STITCH IT IN is a great collection of stitchery how-to, designs and ideas for you, your wardrobe, your apartment and the man in your life. Imagine what you can do for store-bought jeans, vests, tunics, blouses, shirts and ties once you've personalized them with a bit of stitchery. Picture stitchery on a tablecloth, hammock, director's chair, couch throw or pillow.

It's all here with simple, easy-to-follow instructions taking you from the basic stitches to caring for the finished item.

Now you will be able to create a work that is totally your own, a one-of-a-kind masterpiece on each and every item that you choose to enhance.

STITCH IT IN
ARDEN J. NEWSOME

LANCER BOOKS NEW YORK

A LANCER LARCHMONT BOOK

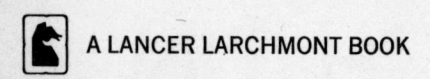

STITCH IT IN

Copyright © 1972 by Arden J. Newsome
All rights reserved
Cover printed in the U.S.A.

LANCER BOOKS, INC. • 1560 BROADWAY
NEW YORK, N.Y. 10036

Introduction		7
Chapter I	TO START	9
Chapter II	DESIGN METHODS	21
Chapter III	THE STITCHES	27
Chapter IV	THE PROJECTS	59
Chapter V	STITCHERY SUPPLIERS	185

Introduction

STITCH IT IN is a great collection of stitchery how-to, designs, ideas and doings for you, your wardrobe, your apartment and the men in your life. Imagine what you can do for store-bought jeans, vests, tunics, blouses, shirts and ties once you've personalized them with a bit of imaginative stitchery. Picture stitchery on a tablecloth, hammock, director's chair, couch throw or pillow. Now you can create for yourself those one-of-a-kind items usually found only in the most exclusive boutiques.

The basics of stitchery are not difficult. The magic of stitchery is in how the stitches, designs, yarn and fabrics are put together. But that's no problem. In this age of anything goes fashions and accessories, you can make stitchery your own personal thing. Make it whatever you want it to be. Put it wherever you want it to go; as simple or as elaborate as you please. After all, you are an important individual, not like anyone else in the world. And half the fun of making it is being you. The other half is creating super stitchery items that tell the world you are you and no one else.

Chapter One

To Start

YARNS AND THREADS

Many embroidery experts believe that certain types of traditional embroideries must use a specific or particular kind of yarn; that certain designs are suitable only for certain fabrics and are not correctly executed and unacceptable unless the proper yarns or thread is used to work the design. So why do you think we now call it stitchery instead of embroidery? Today's stitchery is the product of the new generation. They have broken all the old rules and created a whole batch of exciting ideas. Combinations of yarns, threads, fabrics, stitches and designs have been put together like they were never put together before. The results are sensational. There are no really firm rules for today's stitchery, only those you create and develop yourself. Experience is still the best teacher. You will soon learn the right combination of yarns, threads, fabrics and designs to use to achieve the results you want. Experience will also teach you that if the yarn-threaded needle doesn't pull through the background fabric easily, or the detail of the design is wiped out by the thickness of the yarn, it's time for a change to either finer yarns, a larger needle, a coarser more loosely woven background fabric or a different size design.

You have a wide choice of yarns and threads to pick and choose from for stitchery. Any type of wool or synthetic yarn, embroidery and pearl cotton, mending wool and knitting worsted is stitchery material. Even thick rug yarn and nontarnishing metallic cords are suitable when used for couching.

Especially made for stitchery are crewel yarns and embroidery cotton. Crewel yarn is a very durable twisted two-ply wool yarn that comes in a rainbow of colors. Also available in an equally wide variety of colors is six-strand embroidery cotton. This can be separated into one, two, three or more strands for working stitches. One strand will produce a very fine stitched design, while six strands will give you a more prominent stitch. To separate strands, cut thread to the correct length (a desirable working length is usually about 18 inches). Count the desired number of strands and with one hand, carefully pull them away from the remainder of the strands making sure to hold them securely with the other hand to prevent tangling. Wool yarns of two, three and more plies can also be separated in the same way whenever a finer yarn is desired.

Gold, silver and other metallic yarns are never used to actually stitch with. Because they fray and pull apart easily, metallics are laid on the fabric surface, then secured with thread or yarn stitches.

There is no rule which states you must use just one strand of yarn or thread in your needle. To achieve bold, heavy effects and a variety of textures, several strands of yarn should be threaded into the same needle. However, big and bold stitchery is best worked in large and long stitches on a firm, heavy background fabric, such as burlap or canvas. For unusual color creations, thread needle with several strands of different colors. The result is sometimes surprising.

Whenever you thread more than one strand in the needle, don't double over the strands or the yarn will wear thin at the needle's eye. Experienced stitchers constantly move the needle along the working thread to avoid thin spots.

Choice of yarns and threads and the number of strands to use will depend on the background fabric, the effect or texture desired, the size of the design, the area or spot the design is being put and whether or not you want the finished piece to appear fragile and delicate or bold and bulky. However, the choice of the best yarns or threads is important. The wrong selection can mean the difference between a great stitchery project and one that bombs.

Yarns and threads can also work for you by getting double, even triple duty from one design. Just by stitching a design first in embroidery cotton and then enlarging the design and working it in thick wools on a different background, you can have two very different super stitchery creations. A small flower design worked with three strands of embroidery cotton on a blouse collar will present an entirely different picture than the same flowers enlarged and worked in several strands of knitting yarn on a canvas bag.

FABRICS AND BACKGROUNDS

Just as basic stitchery is as old as our ancestors, so too are many of today's popular fabrics. The calicos, homespuns, burlaps, denims and velvets of yesterday, plus the knits and stretch fabrics of today have never been put to so many fresh and different uses. Denim, once considered a stepchild fabric has really undergone provocative change. Old MacDonald finds it impossible to believe that his bib overalls have become the fashion rage of the city slickers. And they're decorating them with flowers, peace signs, hearts and bugs!

Whether you buy all your clothes, accessories, and linens off the rack or counter, or sew them from scratch, you'll discover that today's fashions and fabrics go well with today's stitchery. Not only solid colors, but the printed fabrics as well shout for needle and yarn and smart stitches.

Again there are no rules as to what background fabrics are right to work on. But it would be wise to give thought to how much wear, tear and laundering the piece will be subject to. Your background fabric should last the life of your stitchery and vise versa. It should determine whether you work the design with a variety of extra special stitches that require a bit more time to execute.

Anything that is to be laundered should be test-washed first. Nothing can be more heartbreaking than a pocket full of pink stitched posies turning all shades of blue when those blue jeans take their first dunking. Good rule: Stitchery should be applied only to background fabrics that are colorfast and preshrunk.

Some fabrics can work for you and make your stitching extra easy. Coarsely woven materials like linens, upholstery fabric, monk's cloth and woolens, have threads that stand out to be counted and followed. With these fabrics and many designs you won't need a transfer. All you will need is a sketch of the stitches you plan to use and the straight fabric threads to follow.

Knits and stretch fabrics that are used to make skivvy shirts, shells, sweatshirts and pajamas will require a little work from you before you apply any stitchery. Because these fabrics stretch out of shape when pulled taut, they require a firm piece of fabric backing wherever the design is to be applied. Use a piece of organdy cut a little larger than the area to be covered by the stitchery design. Baste this piece to the back (wrong side) of the area that is to be worked. Make sure that you do not stretch or pull the background fabric when basting and that you place the straight grain of the backing material in the same direction as the straight grain of the background fabric. When working the design, stitch through both layers of fabric treating the two materials as one. When design is complete, cut away any excess backing material about one-fourth inch outside the stitchery area. When working these stretchy fabrics, it is wise to keep to a single or several single motifs rather than an all over design which would require a full lining of backing material.

Some knits will take stitchery nicely without the use of a backing. These knits are those which are firm with a minimum of stretch. When working with these fabrics, don't use an embroidery hoop and watch your tension—don't pull stitches tight. If possible, try a few sample stitches on a scrap of the fabric just to see if the stitches and fabric are suitable together.

Machine and handknit sweaters and garments, because of their bulk, are handled a little differently. The directions for the method used will be found in the Transferring Designs section.

Printed fabrics are really great for stitchery projects. Striped, checked and polka dot materials provide the lines, outlines and guides for a variety of stitchery designs and techniques. All over flower, paisley and abstract prints will come alive just by picking out some or all of the printed design with stitches. When you use a printed fabric, the design is already there. All you do is add the stitches wherever you wish, in the amount and variety that pleases you. Stitchery may be applied to yard goods before cutting a sewing project or applied to a ready made print.

When adding stitchery to any fabric that will later be hemmed and made into a pillow, wall hanging, etc., bind the raw edges with masking tape to prevent them from fraying. It's a good practice to always work with a piece of fabric several inches larger than is actually needed. When adding stitchery to sections of garments before sewing them together, overcast all raw edges by hand or machine.

COLOR

Color is strictly a personal thing. You make the selections for the designs you stitch. If you are not sure the colors you select will work up well together; get out the crayons, make a tissue paper tracing and color it. If it looks good, feels right and pleases you—it's right.

If you ever think you need help with colors, take a look at your surroundings, in magazines, and fabrics. Colors and color combinations are everywhere. Tip: Don't try to duplicate Mother Nature. She has a paint box that no artist can duplicate exactly.

NEEDLES AND HOW TO THREAD THEM

Crewel and chenille needles are available in a wide range of sizes to accommodate any and all weights and thicknesses of threads and yarns. Try to have a complete assortment at hand.

Crewel needles are short and sharp with long slender eyes that are easily threaded. They come in sizes from 1 to 10 and are very often packaged in an assortment of sizes 3 to 9. The higher the number the finer the needle.

I

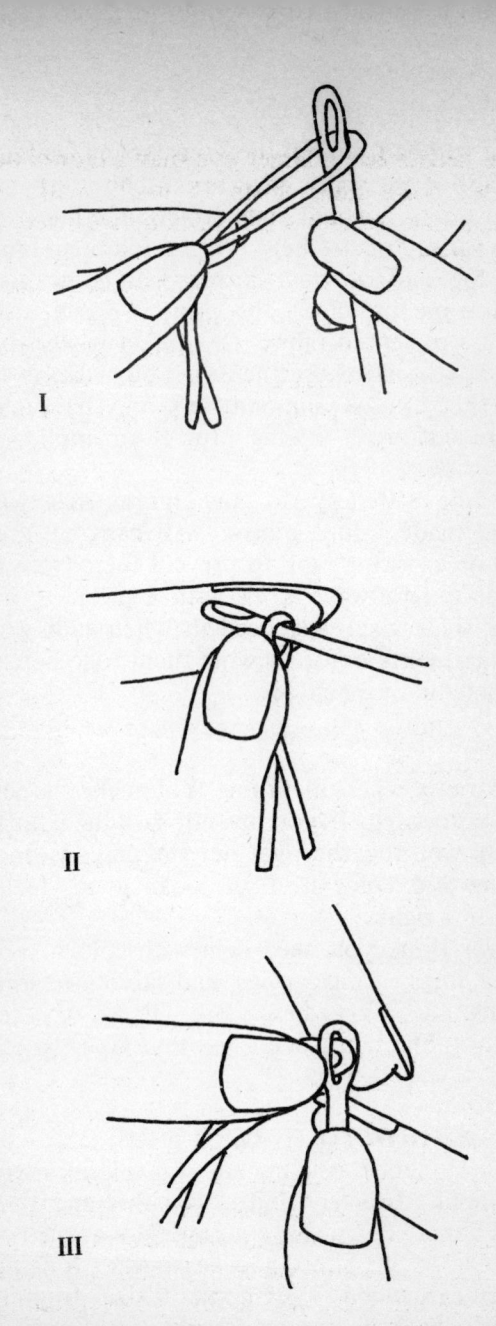

II

III

Figure 1. Threading the needle.

A chenille needle has a larger eye than a crewel needle and is a little shorter. Sizes range from 18 to 22, with 18 being the largest. Use chenille needles when working with very thick yarns or several strands of yarn.

The right size needle for the yarn you are using is the one with an eye large enough to allow the yarn to pass through easily, and the threaded needle to go through fabric without a struggle. If you have trouble threading or pulling the needle through the fabric background, change to a larger needle—but not larger than needed.

Embroidery threads and pearl cotton should enter the eye of the needle easily if you first moisten and flatten the end. Wool yarns are generally stubborn. Handle them as follows *(figure 1):*

I. Wrap the thread around the needle.

II. Hold thread tight and close around the needle then pull the needle away.

III. Squeeze the thread tightly, and press the eye of the needle firmly down onto the folded loop of thread. Then pull the thread through the needle eye.

The correct length for a stitching thread is 18 inches. Anything longer will tangle and knot. Wool yarns especially will fray away and wear thin.

HOOPS AND FRAMES

To use a hoop or not to use a hoop is a very good question. With some purchased ready-mades like hats, handbags and boots, a hoop is impossible. With some fabrics a hoop is more of a hindrance than a help. With some stitches a hoop isn't really needed. On the other hand, stitches like darning, split stitch, satin stitch and laid work are much neater and more accurate when a hoop is used. Whether or not to use a hoop will be strictly up to you. If care is taken not to pull stitches too tight or leave them too loose you can work successfully without one. However, a hoop is a useful piece of equipment and if and when it is possible to use one, you'll find your stitching goes more rhythmically and stitches will look nicer.

The object of a hoop or frame is to hold background fabric

taut and even while you work. An embroidery hoop consists of two rings or ovals made of wood or metal, one fitting inside the other. The most satisfactory ones are made of wood and have a tension screw on the outer ring that can be adjusted to fit the thickness of the fabric being used. This type keeps fabric securely in place once it is mounted in the frame.

Hoops come in a variety of sizes and styles. There are ones that can be held in the hand, others on stands that can be mounted on a table top by means of a table clamp and a large size floor stand hoop. Those with stands are adjustable to a variety of heights, they also leave both hands free to stitch.

To use a hoop, place the fabric over the smaller ring, press the larger ring over the fabric onto the smaller one and tighten the screw slightly. Pull fabric taut but be sure to pull it only on the straight grain and not on the bias, then tighten the screw as tight as you can. When not actually stitching, loosen the screw or remove the hoops completely to prevent marking the fabric.

Generally, hoops are used only for small stitchery pieces, but again there is no set rule. Usually large pieces or projects are worked on a rectangular frame to prevent hoop marks and possible damage or crushing of completed stitchery when moving the hoop from place to place. If you have the floor space or plan to do a great deal of stitchery, a frame is an excellent and practical piece of equipment. These frames and information about them can be obtained from any stitchery shop or needlework department.

A great substitute frame for stitchery can be made from artists' canvas stretchers. These wood strips are available unassembled in a variety of lengths at art supply stores. Assemble the frame by hammering the strips together, paying special attention to getting all the corners square. Lay background fabric right side down on a flat surface, then center the frame face down on the fabric. Pull fabric taut but be sure to pull the fabric threads straight. Turn the excess fabric over the back of the frame. Put a thumbtack at the center of each side, then at the center of the top and bottom. Add more tacks as you pull the fabric, working from the center of each side out toward the corners. If fabric is thick it may be necessary to cut away the excess at each corner of the frame. Put a tack on one side, then another on the opposite side. Continue going back and forth until fabric is secure, straight and as taut as a drum skin. Canvas stretchers should only be used for projects which allow the marks and holes left by the tacks to be cut away or hidden by hems.

OTHER EQUIPMENT

Thimbles — Stitchery can be tough on the fingers, can develop pin pricks, minor stab wounds, callouses and very rough skin on finger tips. If you have never used a thimble then now is the time to try one. A thimble will prevent and protect at least one finger—your middle finger—from these occupational hazards while it helps to push the needle around.

Metal thimbles are less bulky and more durable than bone or plastic. To prevent the needle from slipping when stitching, choose a metal one that is deeply indented. Also, pick one that fits your middle finger comfortably. Try on several, they come in assorted sizes and there is a size to fit you.

Scissors — Any type small, pointed, sharp scissors is a must. Those made especially for embroidery are nice to own, but are entirely optional. A larger pair of scissors or dressmaker's shears will be convenient from time to time for regular cutting.

Tweezers — If you ever goof and find that you must cut and pick out stitches, you'll discover a pair of tweezers very helpful. They will also come in handy for picking out bits of tissue paper tracings caught in stitches.

Plastic Bags and Boxes — When not actually working on them, keep stitchery projects clean in plastics bags large enough to accommodate the project without excess folding. Projects attached to large frames should be covered with a sheet of plastic. Equipment, tools and embroidery cottons can be stored neatly in large plastic refrigerator and shoe boxes.

Magnifying Glass — A small magnifying glass is a great gadget to have on hand whenever you want a closer look at the detail of a pattern, a stitchery photograph or stitchery items on display at museums, craft shows and fairs.

Ruler, tape measure, straight pins, white sewing thread, masking tape and chalk are also supplies you will find useful. Graph paper and tissue paper also will be needed.

MISCELLANEOUS HINTS

There are several helps and hints that stitchers have learned through trial and error and experience. They are gathered together here in hopes that they may answer some of the questions and problems you encounter as you stitch.

- To prevent your left index finger (or right one if you are left-handed), from becoming rough due to constant pricking with the needle, paint finger with colorless nail polish. Rough hard skin will snag yarns and pull at fabrics.
- Before beginning to work, cut skein of embroidery cotton into 18-inch lengths. Place each length between the pages of a book with ends extending beyond the edge of the page. This "filing" system not only prevents tangling, but keeps thread ready for instant use. Unused portions of cotton can be wound around empty thread spools or cardbord rolls cut into short lengths, then stored in a plastic boxes.
- For left handers only: Whenever you have difficulty with a stitch diagram, prop book up in front of a mirror. Then follow the mirror image.
- If you prick your finger and get blood on your work, suck embroidery immediately and the stain will disappear.
- Embroidery cotton has a tendency to twist during working. To remedy this, pull working thread taut, then run the needle down the thread to the surface of your work and up again letting thread untwist. This untwisting may need a little help from your fingers. Wool yarns untwist as you work, so must be retwisted.
- Very often a stitchery design outlives its background fabric especially if worked on a garment that has been worn hard and washed often. If the stitchery design is a single motif, it can usually be salvaged, made into a patch and applied to another background such as a jeans or jacket pocket. To make a patch, see Zodiac Signs, Page 80.

- There is no reason at all why you can't sign your name or initials and date of completion to your stitchery. If it's a piece you're particularly proud of and intend it for the eyes of future generations, you should stitch in your signature. Don't however, sign your name so large that it detracts from the design.
- Stitchery should always be worked in good, bright light. A high-intensity lamp for working at night and on dull days is a good investment.
- Everyone makes an occasional mistake in stitchery. To remove wrong stitches, insert needle, eye first, between the stitches and the fabric. Pull needle upward to raise the stitches away from the fabric, then carefully cut stitches with scissors pressed against the needle. Use tweezers to pick out the cut threads.

CARE OF FINISHED STITCHERY

Washing — Unless the background fabric used must be dry cleaned, all stitchery pieces can be washed. In most cases, like jeans and denims, wash stitchery pieces as you normally would. However, if you care at all about your stitchery, pamper it a bit. Wash by hand with a mild soap, one made especially for woolens and fine fabrics. Soak stitchery item a few minutes. Don't rub, twist, squeeze or wring at any time. Swish gently in water, then rinse well in clear water. Remove article from rinse water and roll it up in towels until moisture is absorbed. Dry as you would any fine garment or sweater. Don't put stitchery items in a dryer.

Transfer Markings — If fabric is washable, transfer markings may come out in the wash. If fabric is wool or unwashable, try cleaning fluid. But use with caution following product instructions. Sometimes it is best to take the piece to a good, reliable dry cleaner.

Ironing — Use a well padded ironing board or suface (cover it with towels). Press with a steam iron or a regular iron and a damp cloth. Place stitchery face down on the ironing board and press lightly working from center out. Don't flatten the stitches. It takes patience, work and some experience to iron a stitchery piece professionally.

Chapter Two

Design Methods

Where To Find Designs — A wide variety of designs appear in this book. They can be used actual size, enlarged or reduced. You can change them to whatever suits you. Combine two different compatible designs and create an all over or larger pattern. Take a section of one design and the section of another and create an entirely different thing. Imagination, a keen eye, awareness and the love of experimenting play major roles in finding and creating your own patterns. Fortunately ideas for designs are everywhere. The circle, for instance, can be the beginning of many designs. It can be worked as is, worked over, built out and worked inside. The same holds true for the square and rectangle. The heart is also a great design starter. Put four together and you've got a flower. Cut one in half and it's blue and broken.

A motif on a paper cup, on dinnerware, a sketch in a magazine, a picture or painting in an art book, a print on wallpaper, a piece of jewelry, a fabric scrap, are all potential designs for stitchery. Several good source for patterns are craft books, children's coloring books and gift wrap paper.

More often than not the design that catches your eye will be elaborate and highly detailed. With some thought and paperwork, even elaborate designs can be adapted to a less complicated outline. Simplicity without too much detail is what to look for when looking for stitchery designs. Graph paper can be a big help when adapting designs. In fact, it can help you to draw your own original things.

Tracing — Designs are traced using tissue paper or vellum tracing paper and a soft pencil. With these materials they can be lifted easily from almost anything. Just put the transparent paper over any design you want to copy. Tape, clip or pin it in place and trace the design with pencil. A tracing paper design is more durable than a tissue paper one and can generally be traced and transferred more than once.

Transferring Designs — There are several methods for getting the design on the fabric. Some methods work on all fabrics, while others do not. Most stitchery experts find and always use the method which works best for them.

Dressmaker's carbon is probably the most popular method used today. Don't however, confuse dressmaker's carbon with typing carbon, they are not the same thing. Typing carbon is taboo. It will smudge, ruin fabric and the black outline will not wash out. Dressmaker's carbon comes in light and dark colors. Use a color that will be seen on the background fabric, but not one that stands out. Tape your background fabric smoothly to a hard, flat surface. Place carbon, colored side down on the fabric, then put the tracing on top; tape in place. Trace over the design with a hard pencil or empty ball point pen (the pen is the best), using enough pressure to transfer all markings clearly. Before removing tracing and carbon, lift up a corner to be sure all parts of the design have been transferred.

If your fabric is light in color and somewhat transparent, lay the fabric smoothly on top of the design and trace it directly onto the fabric with a hard pencil. Keep pencil lines thin and light, as they do not always come out in the wash.

Hot-iron transfer pencils allow you to make your own iron-on transfers. They are available in light and dark colors and are easy to use. First trace the design on tracing paper with a regular pencil. Turn the tracing over to the opposite side and carefully go over all lines with the transfer pencil. Be sure the pencil point is always sharp so that lines are very fine. When transferring the design to fabric, the heat of the iron has a tendency to make the transfer pencil lines spread. What you thought was a fine line could become a broad line when finally on the fabric. Broad lines are difficult to cover up with stitchery, especially when fine threads and yarns are used. And the inks of transfer pencils are equally difficult to remove. To transfer a hot-iron pencil design to fabric, place the transfer, hot-iron pencil side down on the fabric and stamp the design with a medium hot iron. *Do not* glide the iron, instead stamp it straight down, leave it in place for a few seconds, then lift it straight up. It's a wise bird that makes a sample test first with a sample tracing and a scrap of fabric. If the test sample is not clear, the iron is not set at the right temperature. If the test is smudged, you moved the iron.

If you do not wish to create your own design, you will find many suitable contemporary and traditional designs available in printed transfer patterns. These designs are applied to fabric with an iron in the same manner as described for transfer pencils. They are also available at pattern counters, variety and department stores, yarn shops and through mail order outlets.

None of the preceding methods of transferring will work on coarse, nubby or pile-type fabrics. Problem materials require the tissue paper and running stitch technique. First trace the design on tissue paper. Then, stitching around the perimeter of the design, baste tissue paper in place on background fabric. Next, using white sewing thread or another light color thread, outline the design (work right over all the pencil lines), with small running stitches. When finished, carefully tear the tissue paper away leaving the running stitch design on the fabric. This particular method of transferring is an old standard used by stitchers for all types of fabrics. It has many advantages. The tissue paper design can be traced from anywhere and practically anything, then applied directly to the background fabric. Once the running stitch is completed it is there until pulled out. If you change your mind or want to rearrange the design, the stitches can be removed and the fabric used again with a new tracing. Besides being accurate, it will not rub off or become obscure as you work. The fine lines of the running stitch are easily covered with stitchery and those that show after embroidery is complete can be cut, then pulled out with tweezers. And finally, there are never any worries about or problems with carbon smudges or smears or transfer lines showing and not washing out.

The Chinese method of transferring designs to fabric using tissue paper is the best way to handle machine or handknits. Baste the tissue paper design to the fabric. Embroider the entire design over the tissue working through both the paper and the fabric. When finished, carefully tear tissue paper away. Then with patience and tweezers, pick out all the bits and pieces caught in the stitching.

Two other transfer processes you should know are the thread count and canvas methods.

Thread Count Method — This is the real thing. The method Cross Stitch lovers and folk stitchers support. No pattern is transferred, there are no blocks to act as a guide; there are just threads that stand out to be counted.

Evenweave fabrics (same amount of threads to an inch horizontally and vertically), such as linen are used. Burlaps, homespuns and hopsacking which sometimes are evenly woven, but more often not, can also be used for cross stitch. An uneven weave will just alter the shape of the cross slightly and give the design a little different look. If the threads can be seen and counted, then chances are the fabric can be cross stitched.

Designs are worked from a chart. The threads are counted both vertically and horizontally and each cross stitch is worked over a square of 2, 3, or more threads.

Canvas Method — This is also accepted by professionals. It is generally used with fabrics whose threads are not prominent or difficult to count: velvets, velours, felt, plus any other fabric you wish to use. The canvas, known as Penelope or cross stich canvas, comes in several size meshes to suit any size design.

Baste the canvas to the background fabric. Be sure that the horizontal and vertical threads of the canvas match the horizontal and vertical threads of the fabric exactly. (One exception to this rule is felt. It is a matted fabric and has no bias or straight threads.) Make lines of basting stitches around sides and diagonally across canvas from corner to corner. Follow charted design and work cross stitches right over the canvas and into the background. Each stitch is made diagonally over the double mesh of canvas, without catching threads. Work stitches tighter than usual.

When design is complete, remove basting threads. Then carefully draw out the horizontal canvas threads one by one (tweezers will come in handy for this job). Next draw out the vertical threads leaving the cross stitched design on the fabric.

Even if you just follow lines and blocks you can't help but develop quite a few excellent geometric patterns that will be perfect for stitchery.

Enlarging and Reducing—When you find the perfect design, but it is too large or too small, there is an easy way to handle the problem. All you need are a pencil, ruler, tracing paper and plain white or graph paper. To enlarge a design, trace it as is onto tracing paper. Use a ruler and a pencil to mark off squares over the design. Use one-eighth-inch squares for small designs, one-quarter, one-half, and one inch for larger designs. (If the design you wish to enlarge is already a diagram marked off in squares, then skip the previous step.) On another piece of paper, mark off the same number of squares in the desired size. In other words, if the original design is on one-quarter inch squares and you want the design twice as large, then draw it on one-half inch squares. (If you use graph paper, the lines and squares are already marked.) Now copy the outline from the smaller squares in the corresponding larger squares. Whatever you see in every square of the smaller design should be drawn in its corresponding square in the larger size. (See *Figure 2,* page 26.)

To reduce designs, reverse the enlarging procedure.

Photostat shops (any place that develops film), have the equipment to enlarge and reduce designs. There is a fee for this service, but if you have a very special design and not the time or drawing skill, you may choose to have it reproduced professionally.

Figure 2. Enlarging a design.

Chapter Three

The Stitches

There are over 300 stitches and stitch variations for embroidery. You may never learn all of them. Actually, you do not need to know many to produce good stitchery pieces. But the excitement of learning new stitches is one of the great joys of stitchery. The more you learn, the more you'll want to learn and use. And the more combinations you use, the more interesting your designs will become. This book illustrates and uses a selection of the most popular stitches (you can find books devoted to just stitches at your library). It's a good selection to begin with.

Like fabrics and yarns, stitches have undergone a few changes over the past several years. Although the stitches are still basic, they are now used to make the most of designs and accent the fabric. They are often made unusually longer, wider and larger than normal to create a different effect or fill in a space faster. Some are even made upside-down or slanted or loose to create a new variation. Remember, the old rules have been broken. You too can invent new uses and variations if you don't let yourself get tied up in old stitchery methods. Put stitches where and as you like them. Make changes. If you don't like the stitch suggested for a design, then use another. Adapt the design to your own taste. If you don't want to work a design in solid filling and would rather outline the complete pattern in stem stitch, then do it. Stitchery is freedom. It's whatever you like best.

Stitches can be classified. There are outline, border and line stitches, open filling and solid filling, isolated and edging stitches, just to name a few. Some stitches fall into several categories. The stem, chain and split stitches, for instance, are not only outline stitches, but solid fillings as well. Stitches and stitchery are versatile, that's what makes it easy to pick and choose and personalize it.

Although many of the old stitchery rules have been broken, not all of them have been tossed away. There are still a few practical ones that stitchery beginners as well as professionals abide by.

When working stitches, push the needle straight up and down through the fabric. Never slant it as you would when sewing and you'll find stitches will be more accurate and laying where you want them to lay. Don't let stitch diagrams deceive you. They are always drawn as sewing stitches would be illustrated because the step-by-step action of how a working thread behaves and how a stitch is constructed is more informative when illustrated in this way. If illustrated as actually worked—with the needle going straight into and out of the fabric—diagrams would be harder to follow and would show less of the action. If you use a lap, table or free standing hoop, you will find it easier to control this straight up and down action of the needle. These hoops allow you to keep one hand above and one hand below your work.

Never make knots at the end of your working thread. Knots come undone all too easily, then the stitchery comes apart. Knots also make bumps and prevent a piece of stitchery from laying smooth. Begin yoru work by taking three tiny running stitches on the design line toward the starting point, then take a tiny back stitch and begin. The embroidery stitches will cover the running stitches. End your stitching by taking a few tiny back stitches through the last few embroidery stitches on the wrong side, then weave the needle through another stitch or two and clip thread closely.

Don't get up tight about the back of your work. Professionals teach that the back should look as good as the front. The back never looks as good as the front no matter how neat it is. But, it can look neat and it is easier to work without a lot of thread ends getting in the way. And since it doesn't take any extra time to anchor ends in the stitching or ending work at each section instead of carrying a thread from here to there, it's good practice to take the time. As for carrying a working thread from one area of the design to another, as all too many stitchers do, this really isn't a good habit to get into. In the first place, the carried thread often shows through to the right side of the background fabric and destroys the stitchery. Second, if you pull a carried thread just the slightest bit too tight, the fabric will pucker. And third, if you work a design on legs of jeans, you could fall on your face when your big toe gets caught in a carried thread.

Tension plays a big part in stitchery. But this is something that must be learned, it really can't be shown or taught. You must discover how much stretch or give a thread or yarn has. Wool is very springy. It stretches easily, but it always relaxes and when it does, it will pull and pucker fabric if a stitch is pulled too tight. The object is to make stitches so yarn or thread lays naturally on the fabric; firmly but not too tight.

STITCH IT IN will not tell you to get together needle and yarn and a scrap of cloth to practice, practice, practice each individual stitch before you work a stitchery design. Even though this is often a good idea, stitchery practice is boring. Besides, there isn't any reason why you can't learn by doing, especially if you start with simple projects. If you've never done stitchery before, then begin with a project that uses one or just a few quick and easy stitches—like *Doodling* on page 62 or *Falling Leaves* on page 108. You can keep a scrap of cloth by your side to try out a stitch once or twice before you actually work it on a background. This is a good idea and could prove time-saving rather than time consuming. But don't get hung up on perfection at the start. Make it easy and you'll soon make it expert.

Figure 3.

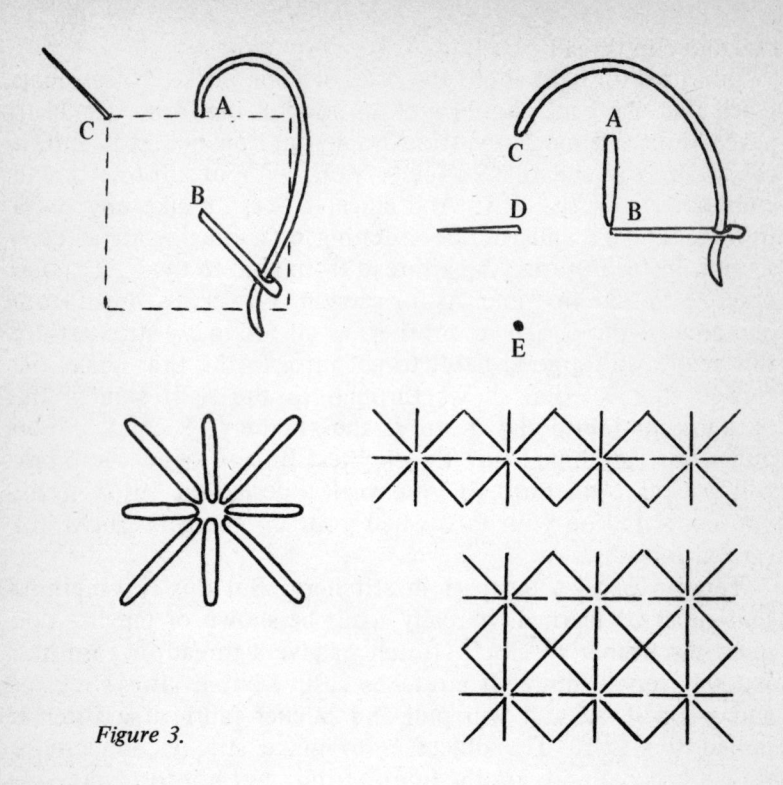

ALGERIAN EYE STITCH *(figure 3)*:

This stitch consists of eight straight stitches arranged in a square.

1. Bring needle up at A. Insert needle at B, in the center of an imaginary square, then bring needle out at corner C.
2. Insert needle again at B. Bring needle out at D, midway between C and E.
3. Make the other 5 arms of the eye in the same manner. Always insert needle at B and bring needle out on the outside edge of the imaginary square.

The Algerian Eye stitch can be used singularly as an isolated stitch, as a border or as a solid filling.

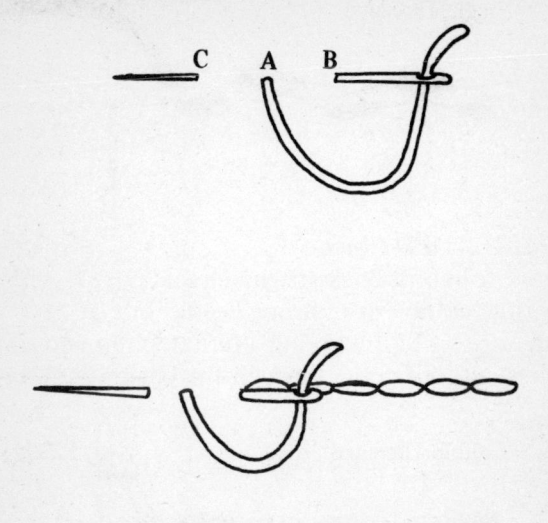

Figure 4.

BACK STITCH *(figure 4):*
The back stitch is usually thought of as a sewing stitch. But it is an easy, very versatile embroidery stitch as well.

1. Come up at A, insert needle at B just a few threads to the right of A, and bring needle out at C, a few threads to the left of A.
2. Continue going back and inserting needle in the same hole as the left end of the previous stitch then bringing needle out a few threads to the left of the working thread.

Use Back Stitch for lines and outlines as well as solid fillings.

THREADED BACK STITCH
This stitch may be worked in several colors. Use it for outlines, especially flower and leaf outlines and for borders. Try threading heavy yarns through back stitch line for an interesting effect.

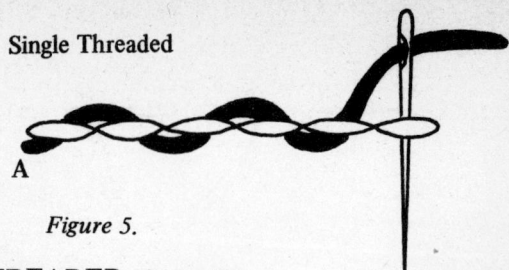

Single Threaded

Figure 5.

SINGLE THREADED *(figure 5)*:

First work a line of back stitch. Thread needle with the same or contrasting color yarn. Bring needle out at A, slip needle under each back stitch, working alternately up and down under back stitches without going through the background fabric.

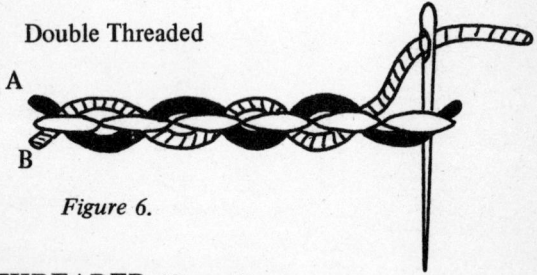

Double Threaded

Figure 6.

DOUBLE THREADED *(figure 6)*:

First work single threaded back stitch. Then take a second thread under the back stitches filling in the openings left by the first threading.

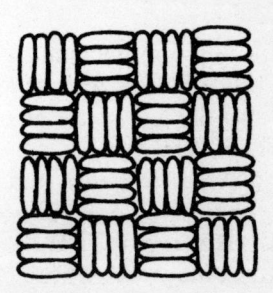

Figure 7.

BASKET STITCH FILLING *(figure 7)*:

This stitch is made by alternating blocks of vertical and

horizontal Satin Stitches (see page 51). Use Basket Stitch Filling for covering large areas. Blocks can have 4, 5, or more stitches but all blocks must have the same number. Try making blocks in two different colors for an interesting checkered effect.

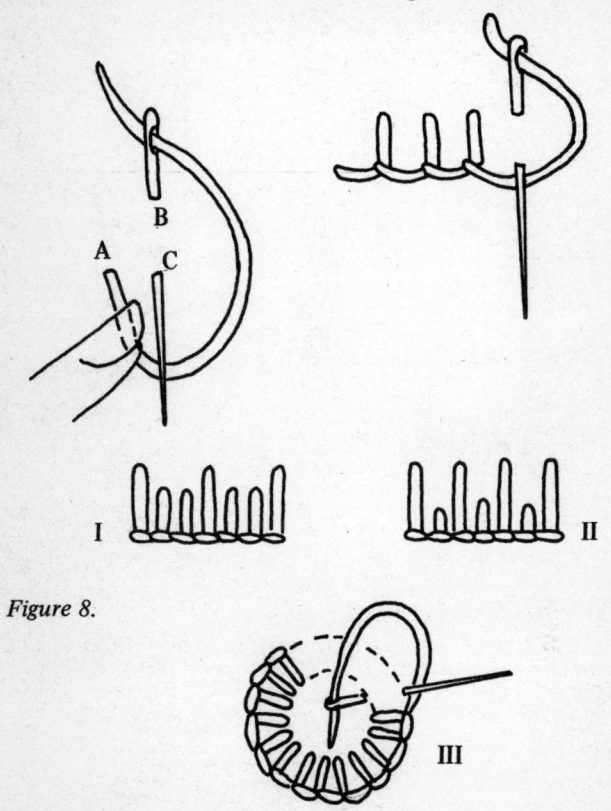

Figure 8.

BLANKET STITCH *(figure 8):*
The Blanket Stitch is usually thought of as an edging stitch that is worked over a raw or hemmed edge. It is a variation of the Button Stitch and is made in the same way, but more widely spaced. A variety of effects may be obtained by altering the depth of the stitches as shown in diagrams I and II. It may also be worked in a circle to produce a flower or spoke shape as shown in diagram III.

1. Bring needle out at A. Hold working thread with thumb.
2. Insert needle at B above and a little to the right of A. Bring needle out at C directly below B. Be sure needle goes over the thread held by thumb.

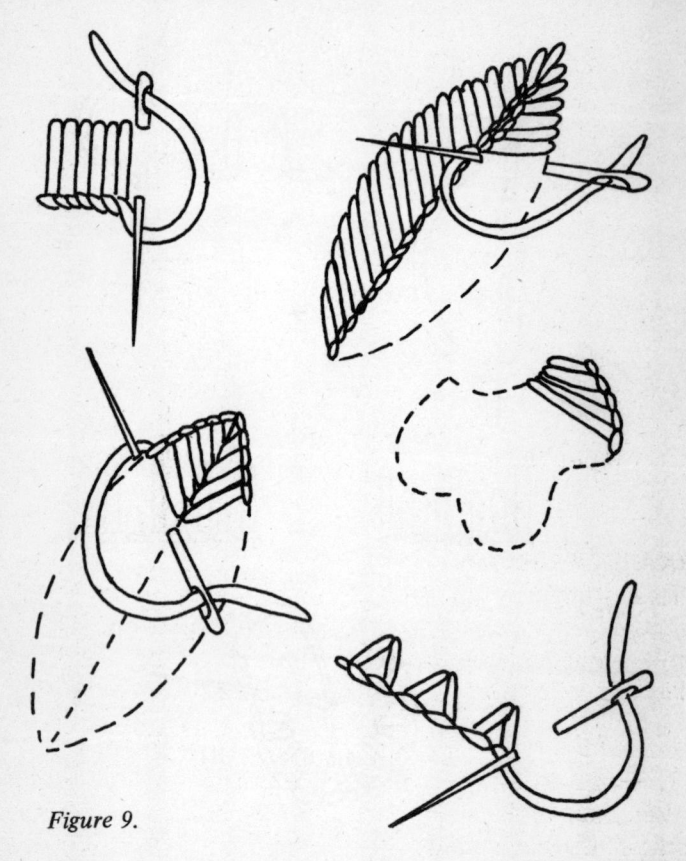

Figure 9.

BUTTONHOLE STITCH *(figure 9):*
The Buttonhole Stitch is worked exactly like the Blanket Stitch, but stitches are worked close together. This stitch is an excellent edging, border, line and ornamental stitch. It is perfect for leaves, flowers and scallop shapes. Because of its popularity among stitchers, many variations and uses have been developed. It's a great stitch to experiment with.

Figure 10

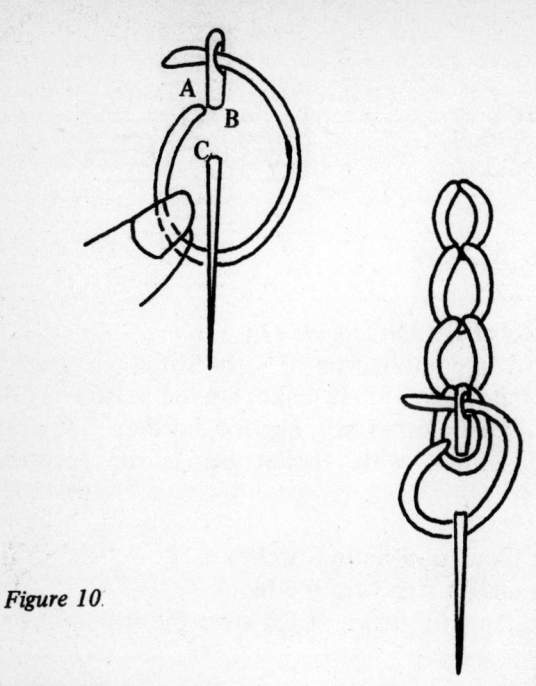

CHAIN STITCH *(figure 10)*:

This stitch is one of the most widely used stitches in embroidery. It can be used for outlines, solid fillings and borders, and with all yarns and threads. It is a quick stitch that takes to curves well.

1. Come up at A. Hold thread with thumb and return needle in the same hole at B, then bring needle out at C (be sure working thread is under the needle), to form a loop on the surface of the background fabric.

Correct tension is important when working this stitch. Worked too tight, fabric will pull and pucker. Worked too loose, the chains will be uneven and sloppy. There are many variations of the chain stitch including the Lazy Daisy Stitch (see page 48) and the Tulip Stitch (see page 56).

Figure 11.

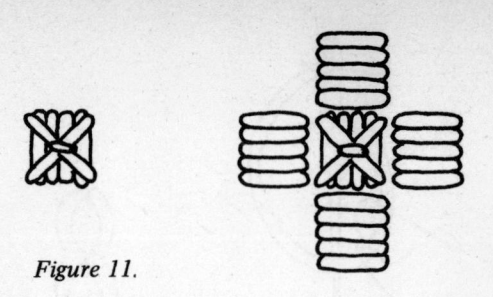

CHESS BOARD FILLING *(figure 11)*:
This stitch is a combination of Satin Stitch (see page 51) and Cross Stitch (see page 39). It makes a good scattered filling and combines well with other stitches for borders. Try combining Chess Board Filling with Basket Stitch for covering areas solidly.

1. Make a block of 4 Satin Stitches.
2. Work a cross stitch over the block.
3. Make a tiny tie down stitch over the intersection of the cross.

THE CHEVRON STITCH *(figure 12)*:
This stitch is great for straight lines and borders. For this reason it should be worked on an even-weave fabric where threads can easily be seen and followed, ensuring straight, evenly spaced stitches. On other fabrics, draw parallel pencil lines and work the Chevron Stitch over the lines. Only practice will make the spacing of this stitch perfect.

1. Come up on lower line at A. Keeping thread below the needle, insert needle on the line a short distance to the right of A at B, then bring needle out at C, midway between A and B.
2. Take needle to the upper line, insert it at D, then bring needle out at E exactly above B. This will produce a diagonal stitch between the two lines.
3. With thread above needle, insert needle at F a short distance from D and bring needle out at D.

Figure 12.

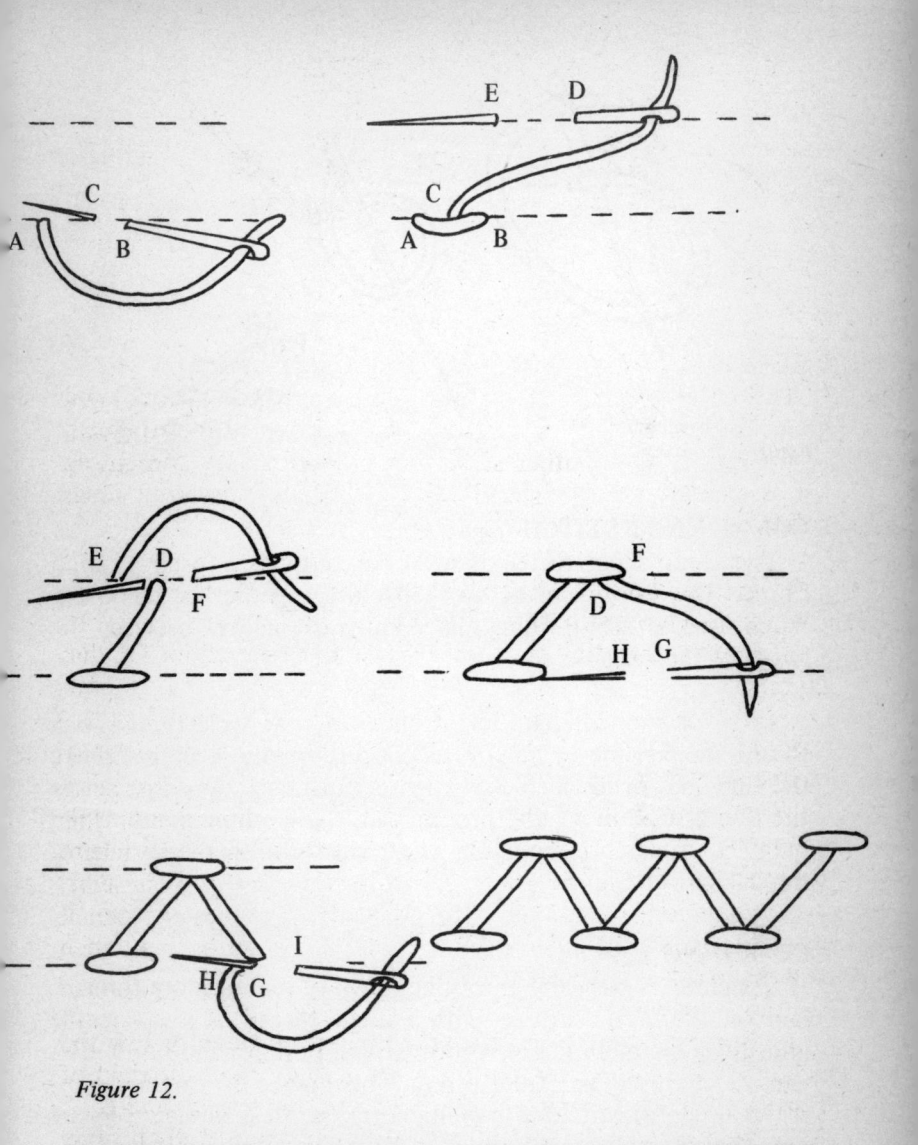

4. Now go down to lower line again and insert needle at G and bring it out at H, exactly below F. This completes the second diagonal stitch.

5. Insert needle at I and bring it out at H. Then go to top line and repeat for second stitch.

Figure 13.

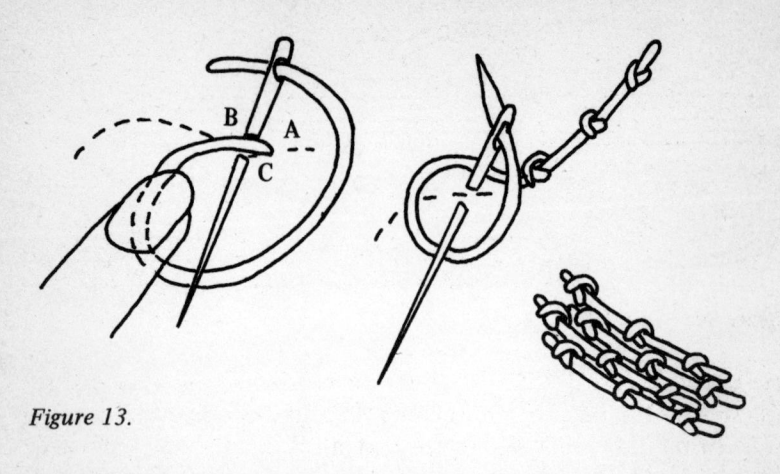

CORAL KNOT STITCH *(figure 13):*
The Coral Knot Stitch is used for outlines as well as solid filling. The knots can be worked close together or far apart. When used as a solid filling, place knots of one row between the knots of the previous row.

1. Work from right to left. Come out at A. Hold thread with thumb on the line to be covered. Insert needle at B, just above the line, and bring needle out a short distance away just below the line at C. Pull needle through over the working thead. When pulled completely through, a knot will form on the surface of the background fabric.

COUCHING *(figure 14):*
Couching is basically the tying down of one or more threads, laid on the fabric surface, with a single thread. It is a versatile and different method for working lines, outlines and borders. It can also be used as a solid filling. Couching is the method most often used for stitching metallic threads on a design. The tie down stitch on couching may be kept almost invisible by using a fine sewing thread in a color to match the yarn or visible by using a contrasting color yarn and embroidery stitches.

1. Threads to be couched are brought through the fabric at

Figure 14.

the beginning of the line to be covered A. These threads are fastened to the back of the fabric with the working thread.

2. Bring the working thread out at B from under the laid threads. Hold the laid threads in place with your thumb, and take tiny straight stitches over them with the working thread. At the end of the row, take all threads to the back of the work and fasten.

Work couching from right to left or from left to right, whatever is easiest for you.

CROSS STITCH

The Cross Stitch is an easy, widely used folk stitch that's as popular today as it was in times gone by. There are several different variations, but the basic cross is still the greatest. And, there are several different ways to do it. Plus a handful of rules for doing it perfectly.

It is important that crosses be regular in shape and size. They must also cross in the same direction. The under thread of every cross always goes from the left bottom corner, up to the top right corner. While the upper thread always goes from the bottom right corner up to the top left corner. All crosses must touch at the corners. To do this, the ends of each cross stitch share the same hole as the stitch adjacent to it. Take special care that all strands of yarns and theads lie smooth and flat. Watch out for twisted strands.

Note: Cross Stitch works nicely on checkered or gingham material where the even blocks form a guide for the stitches.

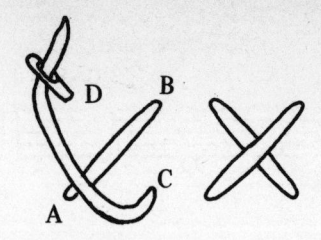

Figure 15.

CROSS STITCH—SINGLE *(figure 15)*:
1. To make a single Cross Stitch, come up at A, insert needle at B, come out at C, then insert needle at D.

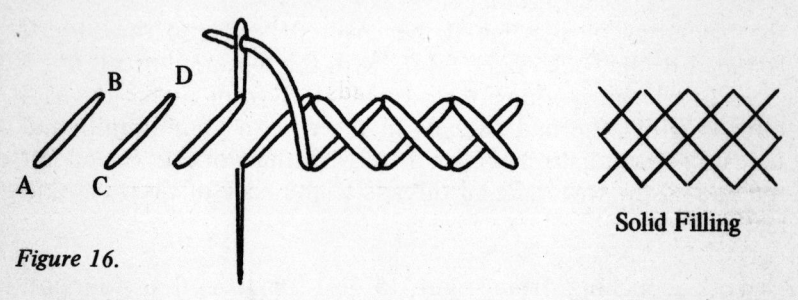

Figure 16.

Solid Filling

Cross stitches are more often used as a solid filling and are worked in 2 trips. *(figure 16)*:

1. Start at A, go down at B, come up at C, then go down at D. Continue in this manner to the end of the row. Then work back again and cross the stitches using the same holes as you did before. The ends of each cross should touch and emerge from the same holes.

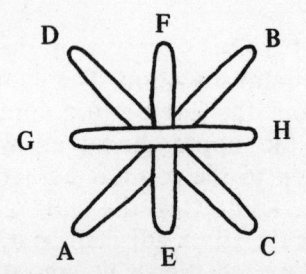

Figure 17.

DOUBLE CROSS STITCH *(figure 17)*:
This variation of the Cross Stitch is an interesting change from the original. It consists of one Cross Stitch worked on top

of another. The Double Cross Stitch can be used as an isolated stitch, as a solid fllling or in rows for borders.

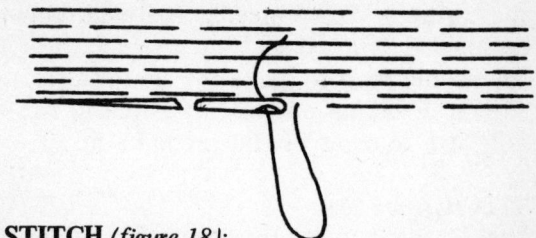

Figure 18.

DARNING STITCH *(figure 18)*:

This is similar to a basting stitch but is used for an entirely different purpose—as a solid filling. It should be worked on a coarse-weave fabric so that threads can be followed to ensure straight lines of stitches and stitches of equal lengths. The Darning Stitch is worked in rows with stitches taken over three, four, or five threads, then under one or two threads—almost like weaving. Work rows close together with stitches placed brick fashion.

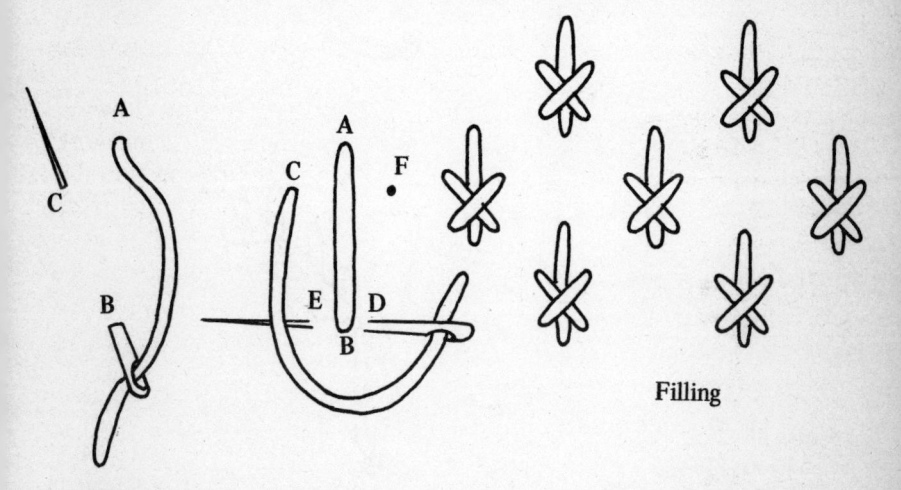

Figure 19.

ERMINE FILLING *(figure 19)*:

The Ermine Filling Stitch is an easy and very effective stitch. It is another variation of the Cross Stitch (see page 39). Try working it in black on a white tie—looks like tiny ermine tails and makes a swinging gift for a guy.

1. Come up at A. Insert needle at B and come out at C to complete a long straight stitch.
2. Insert needle at D to make the first arm of the cross and bring it out at E taking only a tiny stitch in the fabric. Then insert needle at F to complete the second arm.

FERN STITCH *(figure 20):*

This stitch is made up of three straight stitches, all the same length and all using the same hole at the base of each stitch. A quick stitch for stems and, of course, ferns.

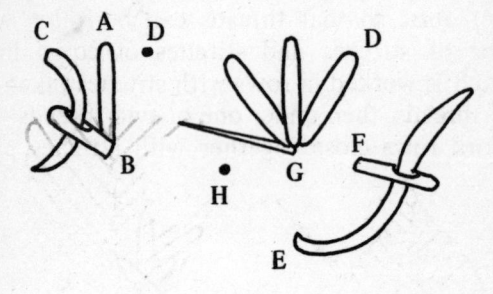

Figure 20.

1. Come out at A, insert needle at B. Come out at C and again insert needle at B. Come out at D and go again into B.
2. Bring needle out at E, insert in F (just a few threads below and to the right of B), and bring it out at G. Then insert needle in E and bring it out at H, then back to E. Repeat.

FISHBONE STITCH *(figure 21)*:

A good stitch for filling in leaf shapes. It looks more complicated than it really is.

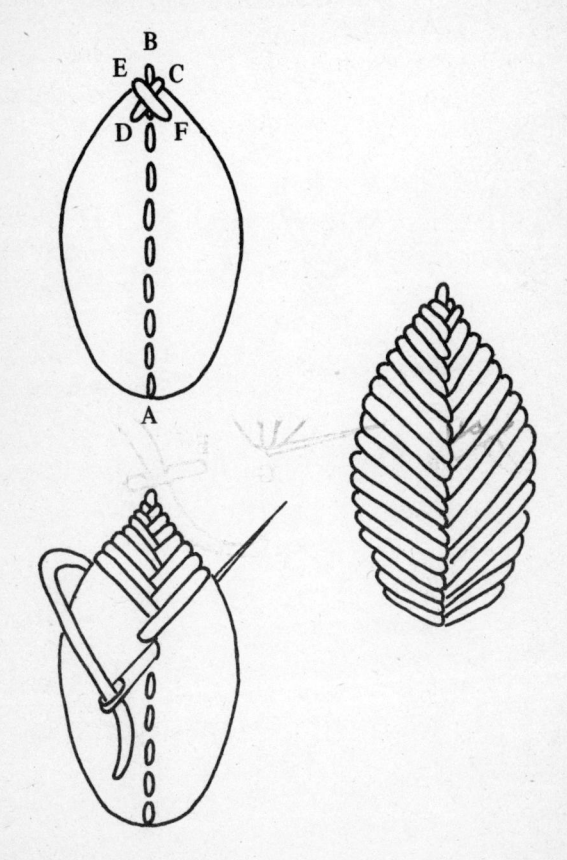

Figure 21.

1. Starting at A, work a line of running stitches through center of leaf from base to tip B. Then bring needle out at C close to the top of the first running stitch, and go down at D just across center line. Come up at E, on the other side of first running stitch, cross over center line and go down at F.

2. Continue to work stitches going back and forth from one side to the other and crossing over the center line. This crossing at the center line gives the appearance of a leaf vein. Keep stitches slanted and close together for best results.

FLY STITCH *(figure 22)*:

This stitch could be called an open Lazy Daisy Stitch. It is very useful and has several variations. Use it in a border, or as a filling stitch.

Tie Down Stitch can be Short or Long

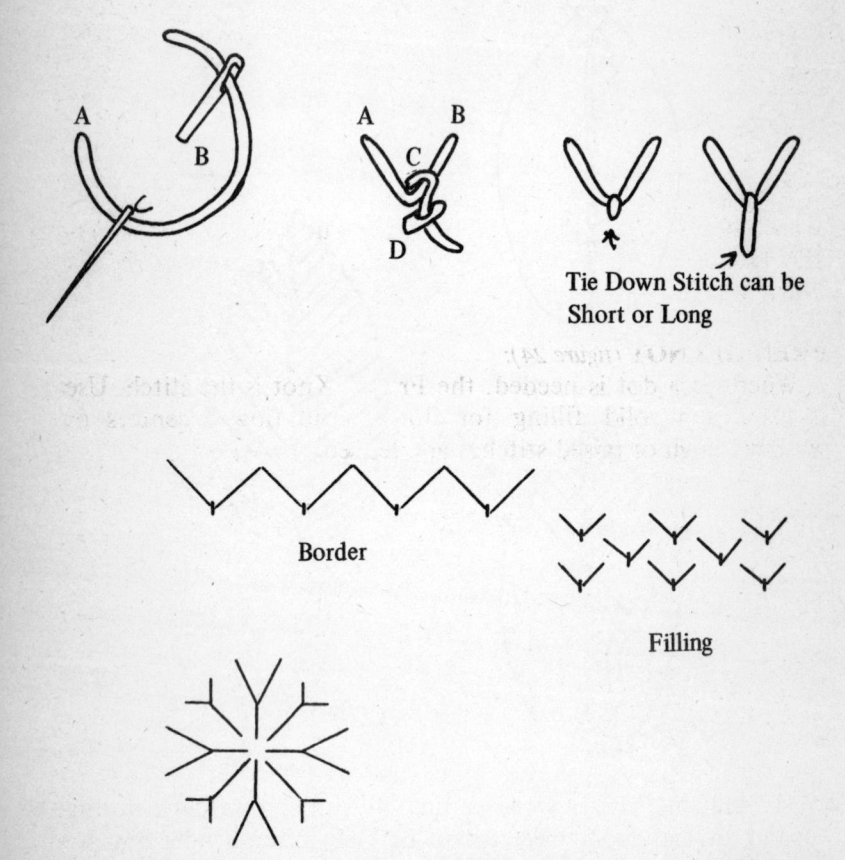

Border

Filling

Figure 22.

1. Come up at A, go down at B, and come out at C midway between A and B. Be sure working thread is under point of needle when emerging at C. This makes a V-shape.
2. Insert needle at D to make tie down stitch.

FLY STITCH, CROSSED *(figure 23)*:
An interesting variation of the Fly Stitch. Great for borders.

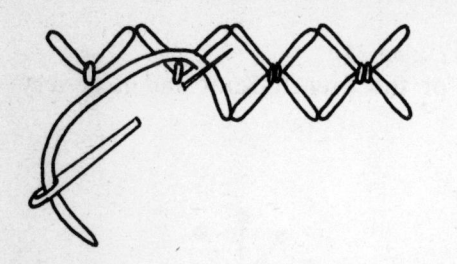

Figure 23.

1. Make one row of Fly Stitch. Turn work upside down and work another row right under the first. Put tie down stitches of the second row, right next to those of the first row to link stitches together.

FRENCH KNOT *(figure 24)*:
Wherever a dot is needed, the French Knot is the stitch. Use it also as a solid filling for flowers and flower centers or wherever high or raised stitches are desired.

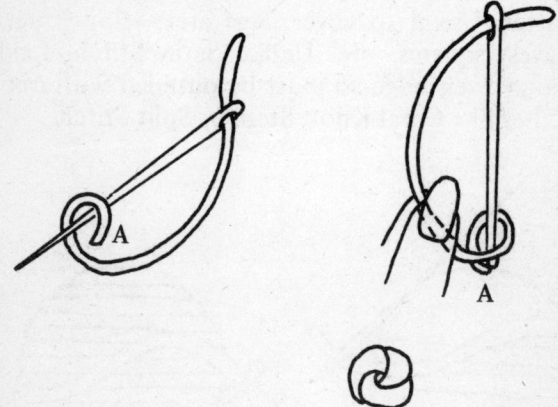

Figure 24.

1. Come up at A. Wrap thread once around the needle.
2. Put needle back into fabric close to where it came up at A.

3. Pull needle through fabric with one hand while thumb and forefinger of the other hand holds working thread taut. Do not release working thread until it is pulled almost through knot.

FRENCH KNOT ON STEM *(figure 25):*
This is just a variation of the French Knot and it is very useful.

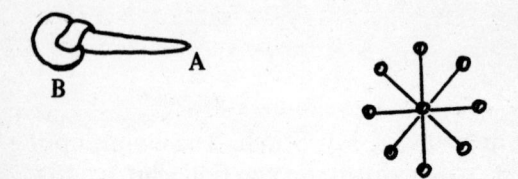

Figure 25.

1. Start same as step 1 of French Knot.
2. Hold working thread taut and insert needle at B, about one quarter inch from A.

LAID WORK *(figure 26)*
This stitch is similar to Satin Stitch but takes less thread and is a bit flatter. Use it to cover large areas—flower petals and centers, leaves, squares, etc. Unlike Satin Stitch, Laid Work rarely gives an even edge so must be outlined with one of the outline stitches like Coral Knot, Stem or Split Stitch.

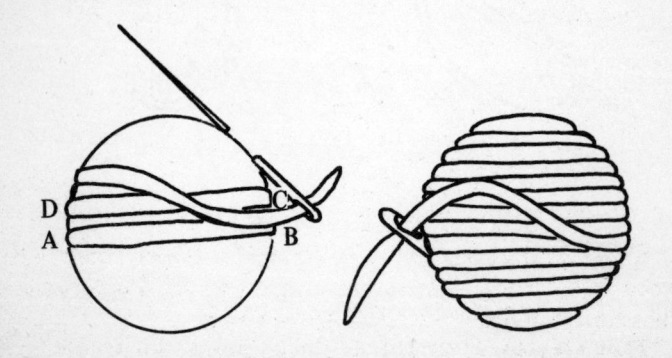

Figure 26.

1. Always start laid work in the center of the area to be covered. Take stitches across area allowing a space the size of thread between each stitch. When end of design is reached, work back again filling the spaces left by the first trip.

2. Work the other half of the area in the same way. You should finish just about where you started with the design completely covered with laid stitches.

For best results, this stitch should be worked in a hoop.

LAID WORK—OPEN FILLING *(figure 27):*

This stitch is one with great possibilities. Experiment with it, use it for large open spaces as well as on smaller areas and flower centers. Try this open filling stitch for covering the complete bib or yoke of a blouse. Work it over pockets and cuffs; be surprised with the beautiful effects.

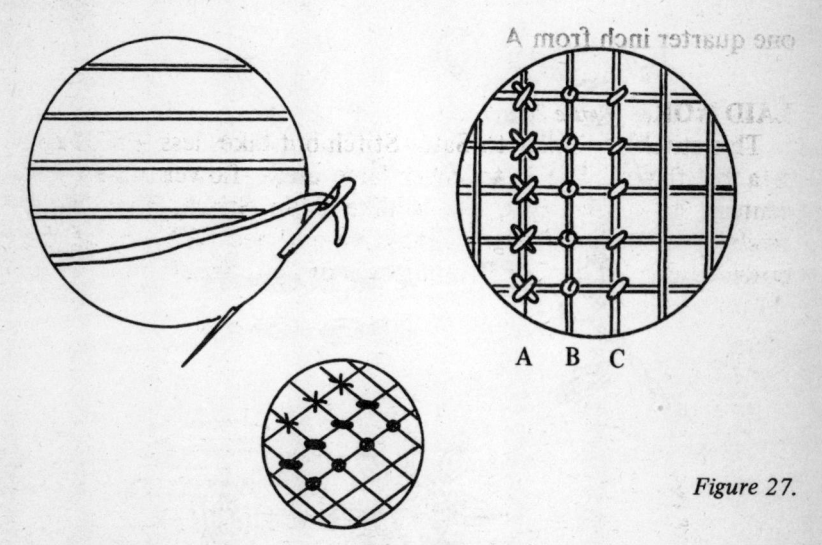

Figure 27.

1. Worked the same as Laid Work but larger spaces are left between stitches and they are not filled in. First, take long stitches horizontally across area to be filled.

2. Then take long stitches vertically across area.

3. Where stitches cross, work a tie down stitch such as the Cross Stitch, French Knot, or Tiny Diagonal Stitch with same

or contrasting thread.
4. Same Open Filling but worked diagonally.

LAZY DAISY STITCH *(figure 28)*:

The Lazy Daisy is actually a single Chain Stitch. It is worked exactly the same except when the loop is formed the needle is taken through the fabric over the end of the loop making a tie down stitch. The needle is then brought out wherever the next daisy loop is to be made.

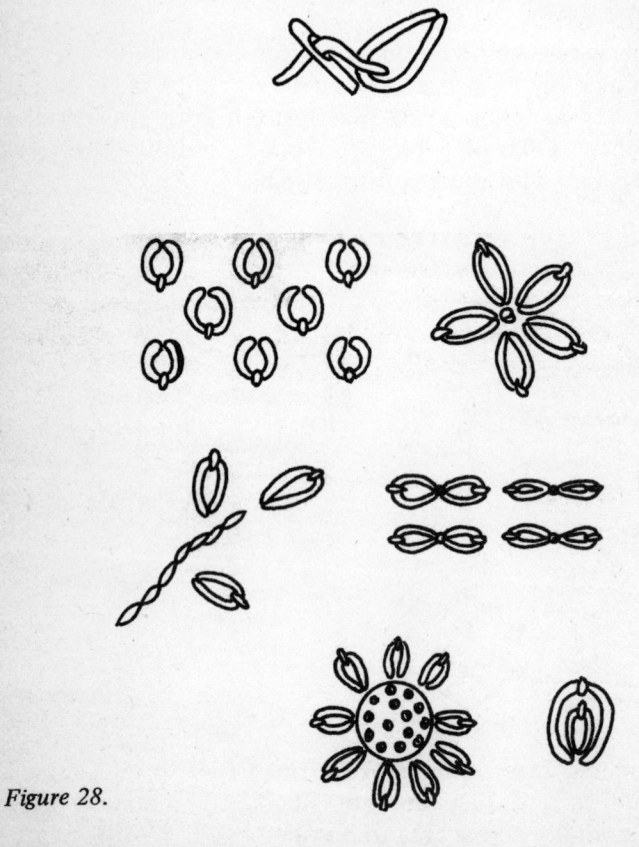

Figure 28.

Use the Lazy Daisy Stitch for leaves, flower petals, or as a scattered filling stitch. It can be arranged in a variety of patterns and used for borders.

LONG-TAILED DAISY STITCH *(figure 29)*:

This is made the same way as the Lazy Daisy Stitch, except the loop section of the stitch is usually made small and the tying down stitch is made into a long tail.

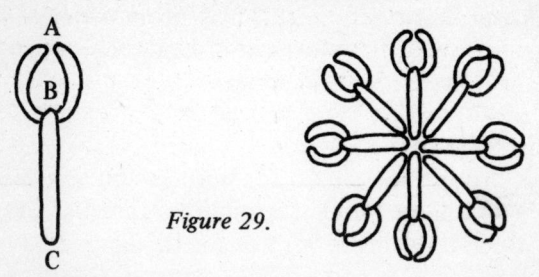

Figure 29.

The Long-Tailed Daisy can be used as a single stitch or as a scattered filling, but is more effective when worked within a circle to form a flower.

PETAL STITCH *(figure 30)*:

This pretty stitch is actually a combination of Lazy Daisy Stitch (see page 48) and Stem Stitch (see page 54). It is very effective as an outline stitch or when worked within a circle to make the petals of a flower.

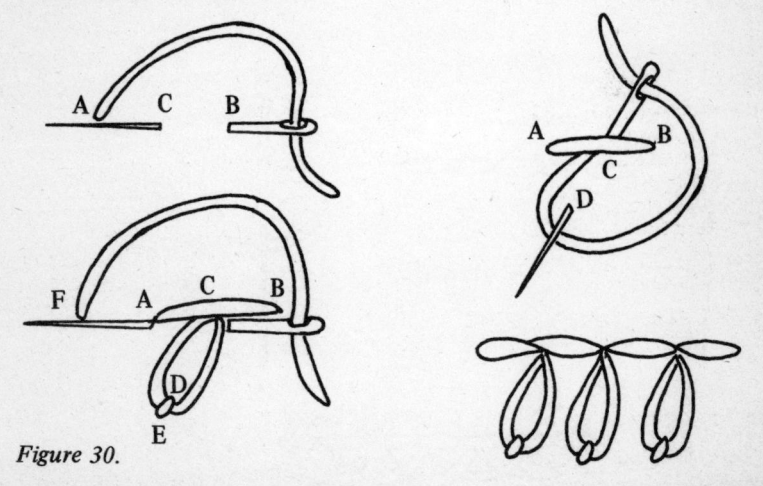

Figure 30.

1. Come up at A, go down at B, a short distance from A. Then come up at C, midway between A and B.

2. Make a Lazy Daisy Stitch to the side of Stem Stitch C-D. The Daisy Stitch should be made at an angle, not straight out from the Stem Stitch.

3. Tie down Daisy Stitch at E and bring needle out at F, a short distance from A. Go down at C again, then come up at A. Make another Daisy Stitch and repeat.

PEKINGESE STITCH *(figure 31)*:

A Chinese stitch that is used for borders and as a solid filling. It is also an excellent stitch for metallic threads. Use metallic threads for the interlacing loops not for the Back Stitch.

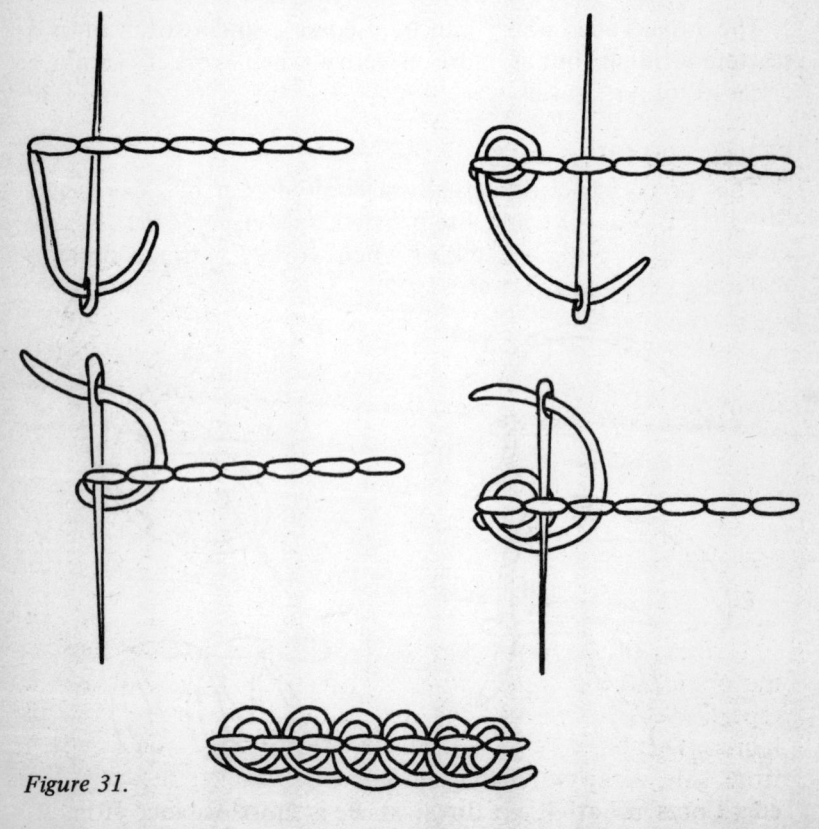

Figure 31.

1. Work a foundation row of Back Stitch first.

2. Interlace the same or contrasting color yarn through the Back Stitches as shown. When interlacing and making the loops, do not pick up any background fabric, just slip the needle under the Back Stitches.

SATIN STITCH *(figure 32):*
Of all embroidery stitches, the Satin Stitch is one of the most popular and versatile. It is a great solid covering stitch for small open areas. Large spaces can also be covered with Satin Stitch, if the area is broken up into small sections. Then Satin Stitch is worked over the smaller individual areas.

Figure 32.

1. Bring needle up at A, at edge of design, go down at B on the opposite side of the design. Come up at C, go down at D; repeat. Working thread is carried across design underneath the fabric. The back side of the stitch looks very much like the front side. Keep stitches close together; don't pull tight; keep edges neat. The Satin Stitch can be worked in any direction; slanted, horizontal or vertical.

SEEDING STITCH *(figure 33)*:
For a nice, effective flat filling stitch, there is nothing as easy or as nice as this tiny stitch. Scatter Seeding all over open areas putting them in random directions.

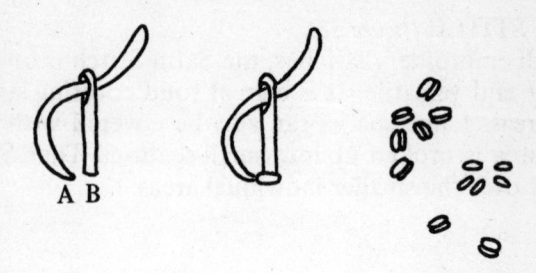

Figure 33.

1. Make two very small straight stitches side by side, or one on top of the other. The latter method will give the stitch a slightly rounded effect.

RAISED SEEDING STITCH *(figure 34)*:
This is a variation of the Seeding Stitch. It is worked in exactly the same way, except the thread is not pulled all the way through the fabric nor is the stitch pulled flat. Instead, a little loop of thread is left on the background surface. Wonderful stitch for furry effects or for duplicating flowers like Goldenrod that grow in clusters. Work the stitch close together or a bit separated, depending on the effect you wish to create.

Figure 34.

1. Come up at A, go down at B, just a few threads away from A, leaving a tiny loop on top of the fabric.

SHEAF STITCH, FILLING *(figure 35)*:
A good stitch to use for scattered filling. Also nice set close together in rows for borders.

Scattered Filling

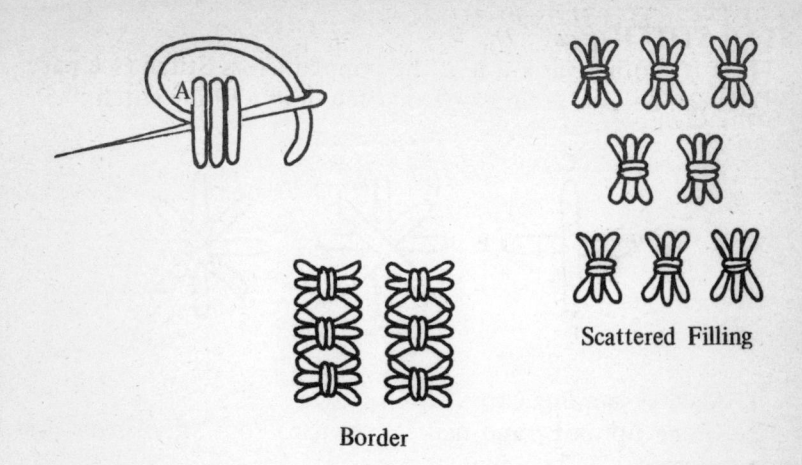

Border

Figure 35.

1. Make 3 Satin Stitches (see page 51). Then bring needle up at center of left side at A. Tie stitches together around the middle with 2 overcast stitches, but do not pick up any fabric. Insert needle back at A.

SPLIT STITCH *(figure 36):*

Split Stitch looks somewhat like a Chain Stitch, but is finer and more delicate. It's a good outline stitch as well as a solid filing stitch. Use only yarns when working this stitch; embroidery cottons cannot be split to achieve the desired effect.

Figure 36.

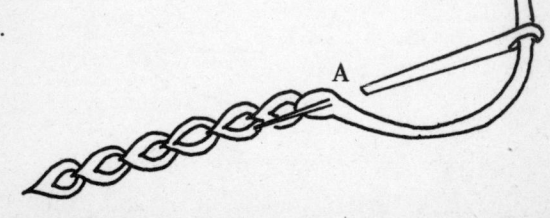

1. The Split Stitch is worked almost in the same way as Stem Stitch except the needle goes through—or splits—the working thread as it comes out at A.

STAR STITCH *(figure 37):*

This is another variation of the popular Cross Stitch (see page 39). It can be used as an isolated stitch or as a filling stitch.

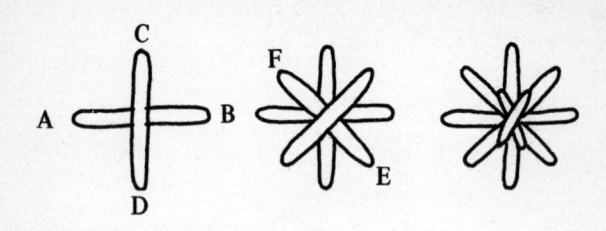

1. Make a standing Cross Stitch.
2. Come up at E, and make a regular Cross Stitch over the upright cross.
3. Come up at F between the spokes of the double cross and make a small oblong cross over the intersection of the first two crosses.

STEM STITCH *(figure 38):*

This popular stitch is also called Outline Stitch and Crewel Stitch. It is often used for outlines and solid filling. When using Stem Stitch as an outline stitch, keep thread above the needle. This will produce a straighter line. When using this stitch as a solid filling, work rows close together, side by side.

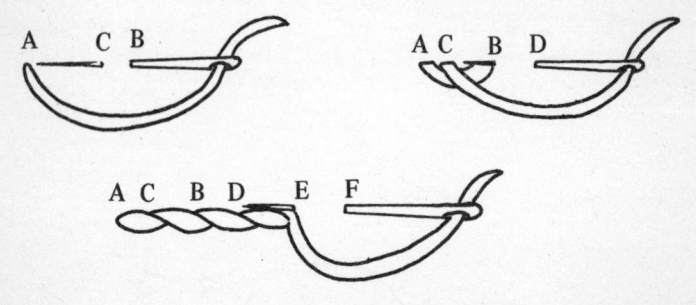

1. Come up at A, insert needle at B and come up at C, halfway between A and B. Hold thread below needle.
2. Insert needle at D, come up in B; continue, repeating Step 2.

STRAIGHT STITCH *(figure 39)*:

This stitch is exactly what the name implies—straight. It is one of the easiest stitches to do and can be made in any direction and in any length. When made extra long, tie Straight Stitch down with tiny Straight Stitches.

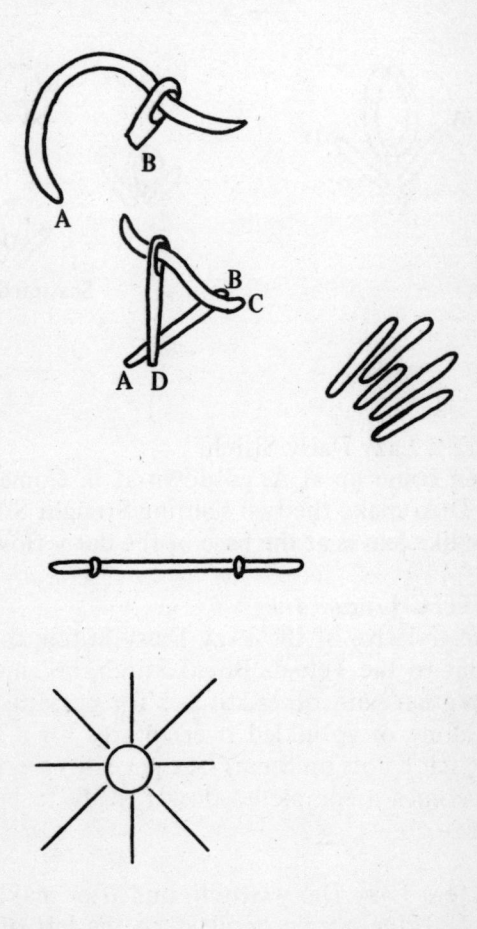

1. Come up at A, go down at B.
2. Come up at C and go down at D.

TETE-DE-BOEUF STITCH *(figure 40)*:

This is one stitch that is a design in itself. It is a beautiful scattered filling stitch, as well as an isolated stitch. The Tete-de-Boeuf Stitch is a combination of the Lazy Daisy Stitch (see page 48) and the Straight Stitch (see page 55).

Scattered Filling

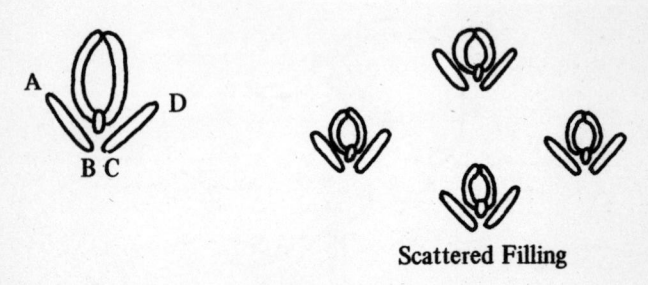

Figure 40.

1. Make a Lazy Daisy Stitch.
2. Then come up at A, go down at B. Come up at C and go down at D to make the two slanting Straight Stitches that form two spike-like leaves at the base of the daisy flower.

TULIP STITCH *(figure 41)*:

Another relative of the Lazy Daisy Stitch, the Tulip Stitch is also similar to the Tete-de-Boeuf Stitch, but more elaborate. It works up great with other stitches for peasant-like border, can be used alone or sprinkled over an area for a scattered filling. When French Knots on Stems (see page 46) are added, the Tulip Stitch becomes a completed flower ready to be used wherever you want it.

1. Make a Lazy Daisy Stitch, but after making the tie down stitch at C, bring needle up at D, to the left of the loop about midway between A-B.
2. From D, slip the needle under the tie down stitch, pull yarn through—but not too tight—and insert needle on the other side of the loop at E. Repeat for another arm, making it just a

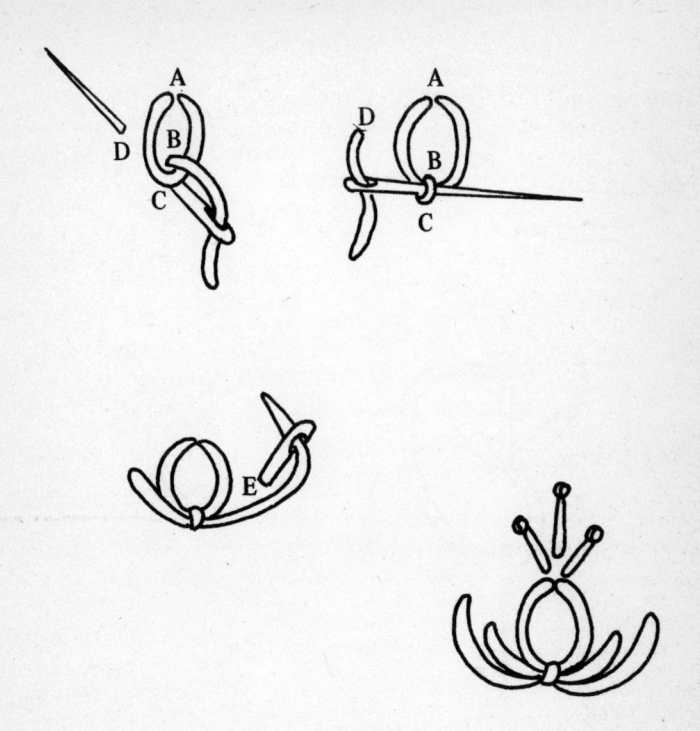

Figure 41.

little longer than the first arm. These arms can be worked in a different color than the Lazy Daisy Stitch.

WHEAT EAR STITCH, DETACHED *(figure 42):*

This scattered filling stitch is similar to one known as a broadline Wheat Ear Stitch. However, it is made slightly different. This Wheat Ear Stitch is another member of the Lazy Daisy and the Straight Stitch family.

1. Come up at A, go down at B, then come out at C and go down again at A to complete ears.
2. Work a Lazy Daisy Stitch over the ears.

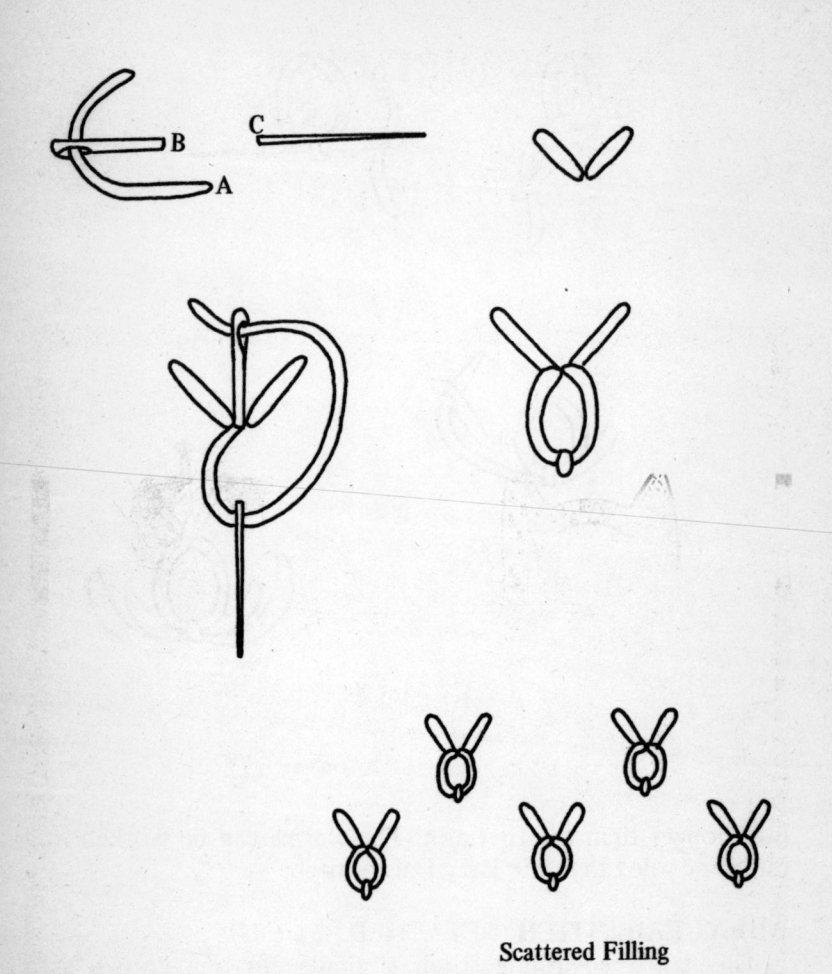

Figure 42. Wheat Ear Stitch, detached.

Chapter Four

The Projects

Figure 43. Happy Cat.

HAPPY CAT WALL HANGING *(figure 43)*:

Kittenish way to practice 16 different stitches until purr-fect. Materials: 28 inch x 28 inch piece of coarse-weave background fabric (linen, lightweight upholstery fabric, homespun); knitting yarn in various weights and colors; assorted crewel needles; canvas stretchers; large sheet of paper for enlarging design (white shelf paper is good); pencil; ruler; wood stapler.

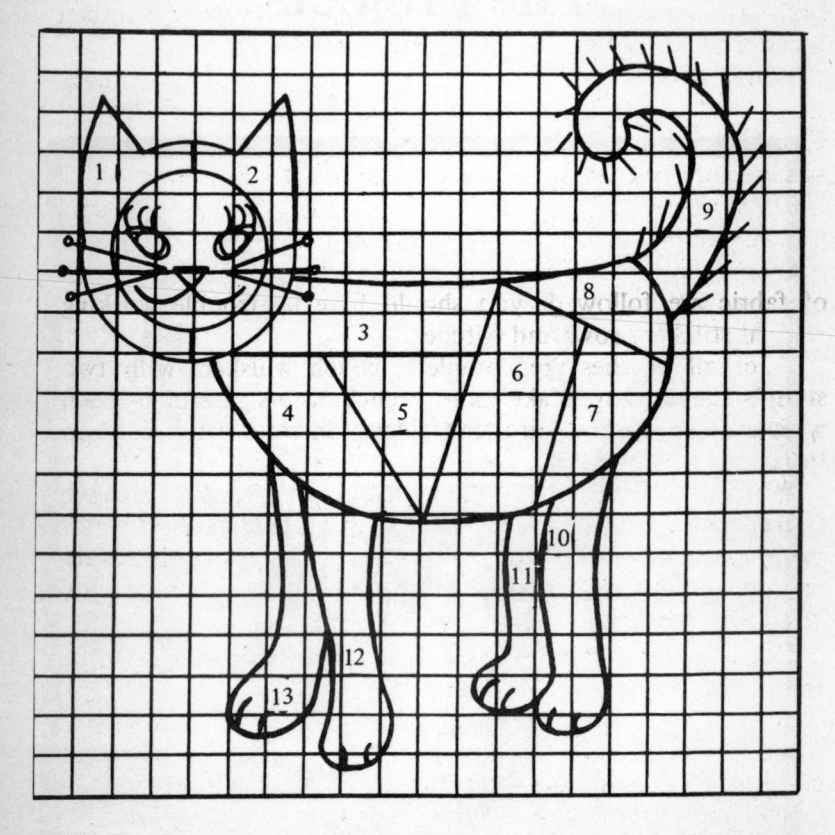

Figure 44. Stitch Key: (1) Seeding. (2) Tete-de-boeuf stitch. (3) Algerian eye stitch. (4) Laid work–open filling with cross. (5) Split stitch. (6) Ermine filling. (7) Chain stitch. (8) Fly stitch filling. (9) Stem stitch. (10) Coral stitch filling. (11) Darning stitch. (12) Lazy daisy stitch. (13) Sheaf stitch filling. Each square equals one inch.

Directions: Enlarge pattern of cat by copying on large sheet of paper ruled off in one-inch squares. Transfer enlarged design to center of background fabric using transfer method best suited for your fabric (*Figure 44*).

Assemble canvas stretchers to make a frame 23 inches x 23 inches. Canvas stretchers come in assorted sizes from 8 inches to 60 inches. The lengths are interchangable to make any size or shape frame you need. Stretch fabric over frame; bring excess to back and staple with wood stapler (see page 16). Be sure design is centered and threads of fabric are pulled straight.

Couch all lines except eyes, nose, whiskers and paw markings, using two strands of black 4-ply knitting worsted. When all Couching is complete, embroider nose in Satin Stitch, eye outline and lashes in Stem Stitch, pupil in Satin Stitch.

Following stitch key, embroider patches working each in a different color and type or weight of yarn. All patches are filled with open, powdered or solid filling stitches. If straight threads of fabric are followed, you should have no trouble working straight stitchery rows and stitches.

After all patches are complete, couch whiskers with two strands black yarn. Make large French Knots at end of each whisker. Paw markings are embroidered in stem stitch right on top of the filling stitches.

When embroidery is complete, remove staples and restretch background fabric if necessary. If fabric is still taut, it is not necessary to remove it from the frame. If yarn is slightly soiled, brush over the surface with a clean cloth dipped in a good cleaning fluid. This sometimes helps to freshen colors.

Cut a piece of heavy brown paper slightly smaller than the frame, and glue it over the back of the frame.

A wood strip picture frame can be added if desired. Cut wood stripping (available from lumber yard), to fit sides, top and bottom of your stitchery picture. Be sure to miter corners (you'll need a saw and a miter box and possibly a little help from a friend).

Stain wood strips with brown liquid shoe polish. Nail stripping to stretcher frame. Countersink nails and fill holes with plastic wood (a wood filler). Stain wood filler with shoe

DOODLES *(figures 45a and b):*

You doodle. Your favorite people doodle. Put them all together, then easy stitch them in Back Stitch, Straight Stitch and French Knots. Make them in white on a black background, or in black on a white background. How about a combination of hot pink, electric yellow, blazing green and white? Doodles fit anywhere and anything—jeans, sneakers, bags, vests. And doodles are exclusively yours.

Materials: Background fabric (anything you want it to be that is stitchable); yarns or embroidery cotton in your choice of colors (weights will depend on the background fabric); crewel needle; scissors; tissue paper.

Figure 45a.

Figure 45b.

Directions: Trace doodles actual size or enlarge them. Transfer doodle designs to background fabric. Scatter them all over. Work all short straight lines in Straight Stitch, all other lines in back stitch; dots in French Knots. (Not ready for French Knots? Then work dots in seeding stitch.)

Top: **Happy Cat Wall Hanging is a great way to practice sixteen different stitches. (See page 60.)**

Bottom: **Peasant Belt with Hanging Pocket—This beautiful design will enhance any accessory. (See page 128.)**

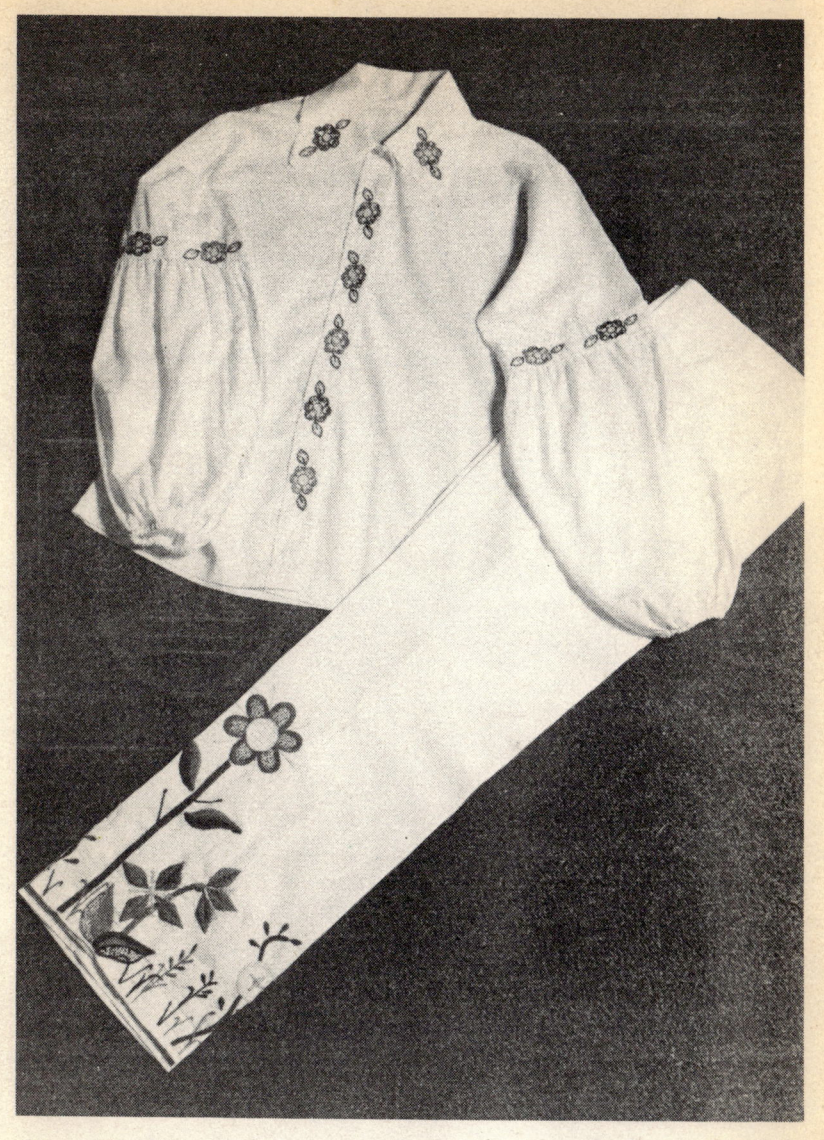

Top: One Flower—A single flower motif stitched around buttonholes, on collar and sleeves adds an interesting accent. (See page 89.)

Bottom: In A Flower Garden grows up your leg when you pick the right spot and plant stitches with loving care. (See page 115.)

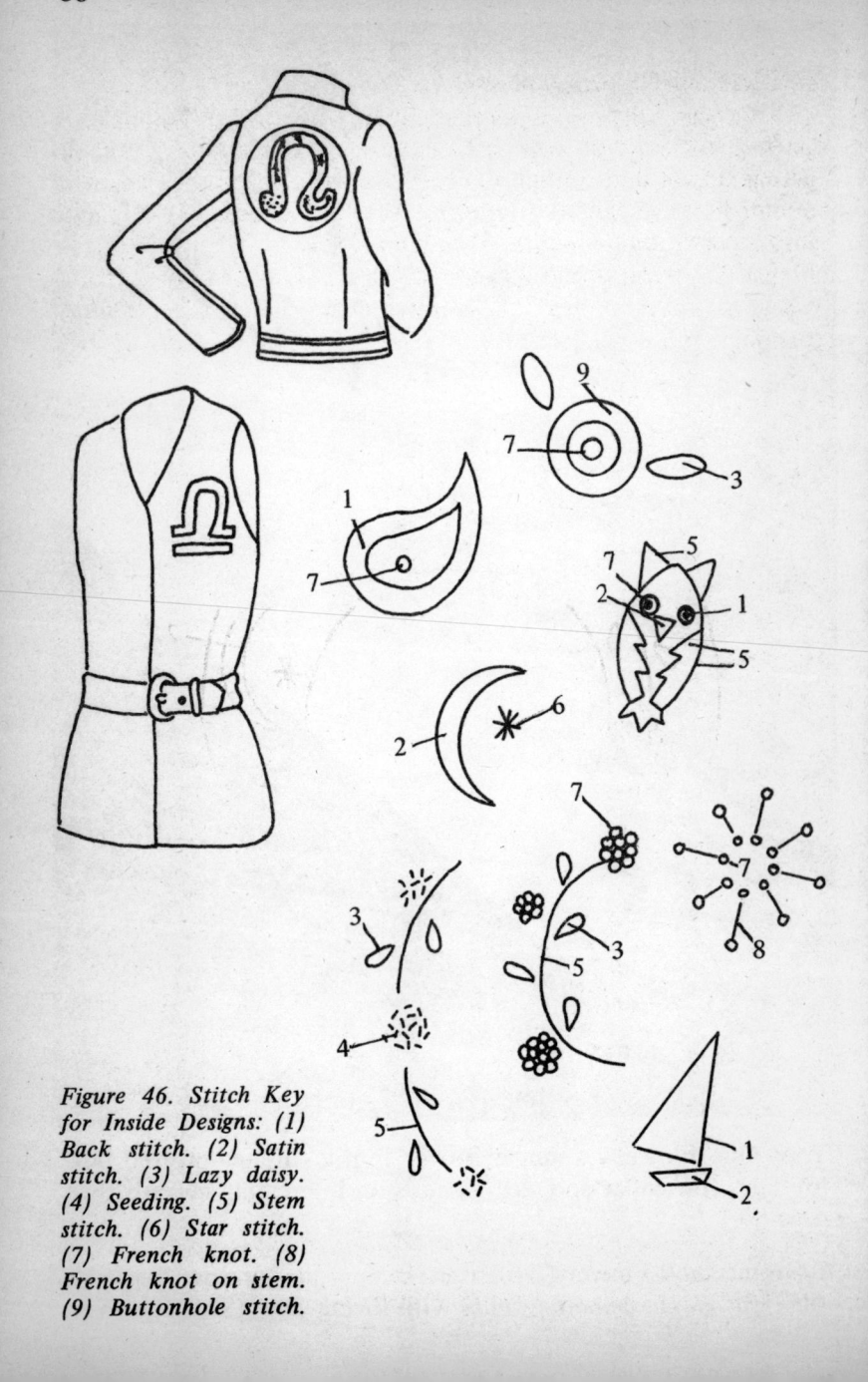

Figure 46. Stitch Key for Inside Designs: (1) Back stitch. (2) Satin stitch. (3) Lazy daisy. (4) Seeding. (5) Stem stitch. (6) Star stitch. (7) French knot. (8) French knot on stem. (9) Buttonhole stitch.

ZODIAC SIGNS *(figures 46, 47a–l):*

Your sign where you want it. Sport yours or his zodiac on a pocket, the seat of your pants, the front of his vest. Do it up actual size or do it up big. Large size goes great on the back of a denim battle jacket or the front of a big canvas bag. Make it into a patch, then applique it on your sleeve.

Materials: Background fabric; crewel yarn or 3-play knitting yarn in your choice of colors, plus the usual stitchery paraphernalia.

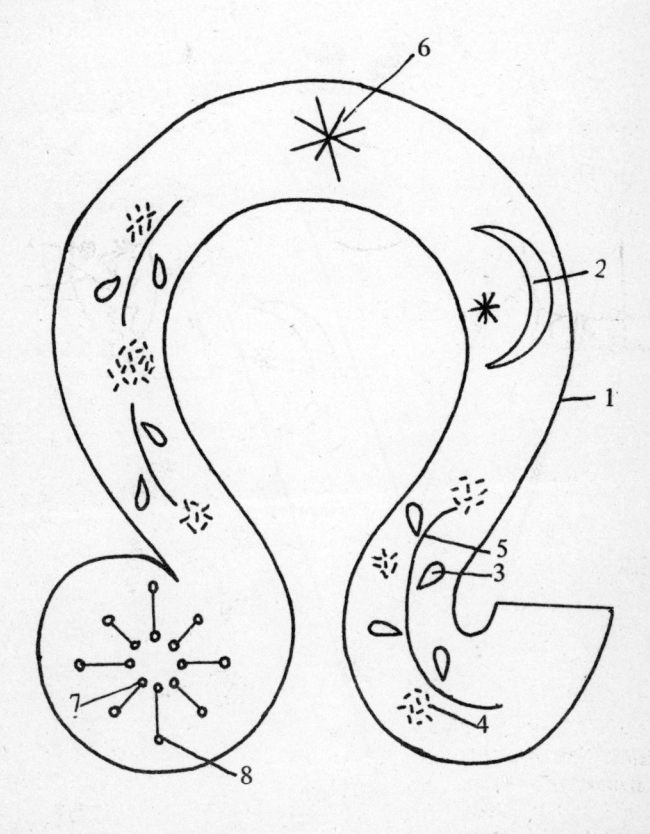

Figure 47a. Stitch Key for Leo (July 23–August 23) Zodiac Sign: (1) Coral knot stitch. (2) Satin stitch. (3) Lazy daisy. (4) Seeding. (5) Stem stitch. (6) Star stitch. (7) French knot. (8) French knot on stem.

Directions: Trace actual size design. Transfer to background fabric. Embroider all zodiac signs following stitch keys. Make changes in stitches if desired. Try substituting Stem Stitch for Coral Knot Stitch, French Knot for Raised Seeding. Create different designs within the zodiac outline—Lazy Daisy flowers, tiny paisleys in Back Stitch. You be the creator. (See Leo sign for inspiration (*figure 47a*).

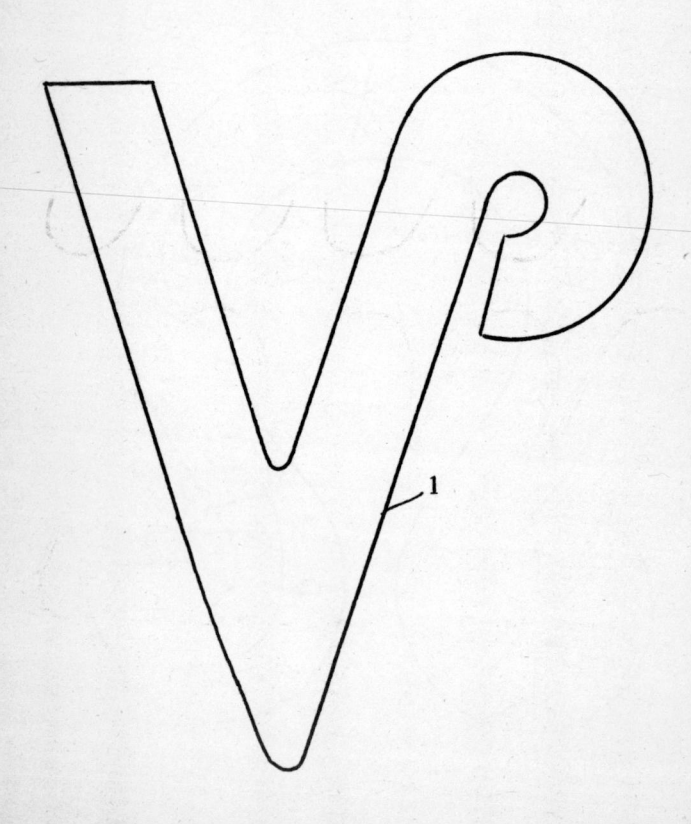

Figure 47b. Stitch Key for Capricorn (Dec. 21–Jan. 20) Zodiac Sign: (1) Coral Knot Stitch.

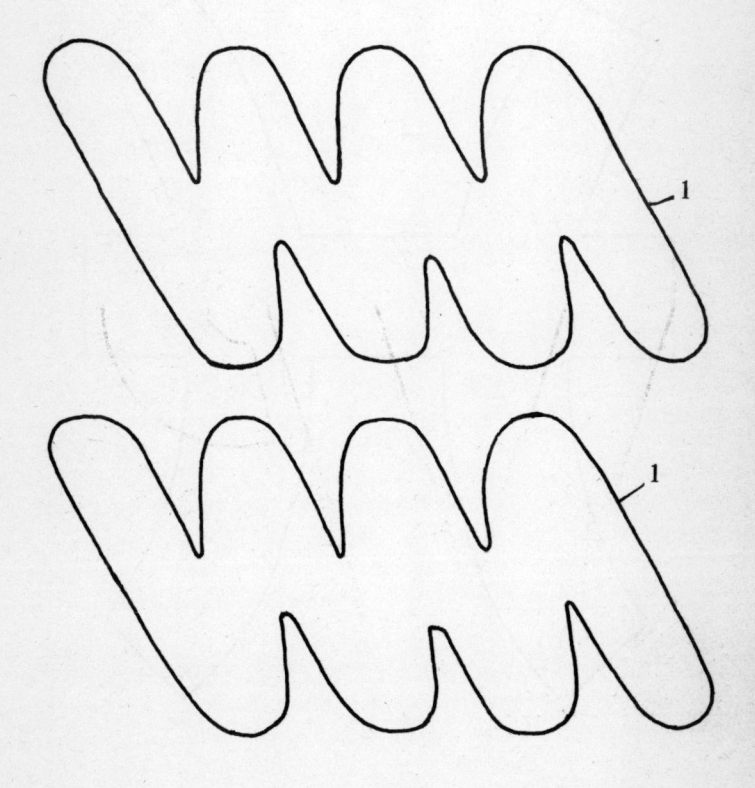

Figure 47c. Stitch Key for Aquarius (Jan. 20–Feb. 19) Zodiac Sign: (1) Coral Knot Stitch.

70

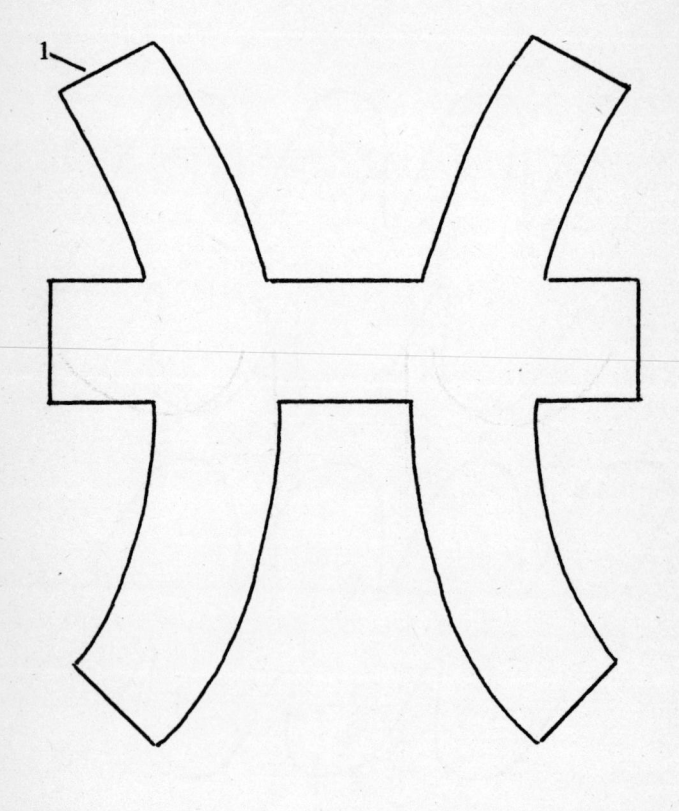

Figure 47d. Stitch Key for Pisces (Feb. 19–March 20) Zodiac Sign: (1) Coral Knot Stitch.

Figure 47e. Stitch Key for Aries (March 20–April 20) Zodiac Sign: (1) Coral Knot Stitch.

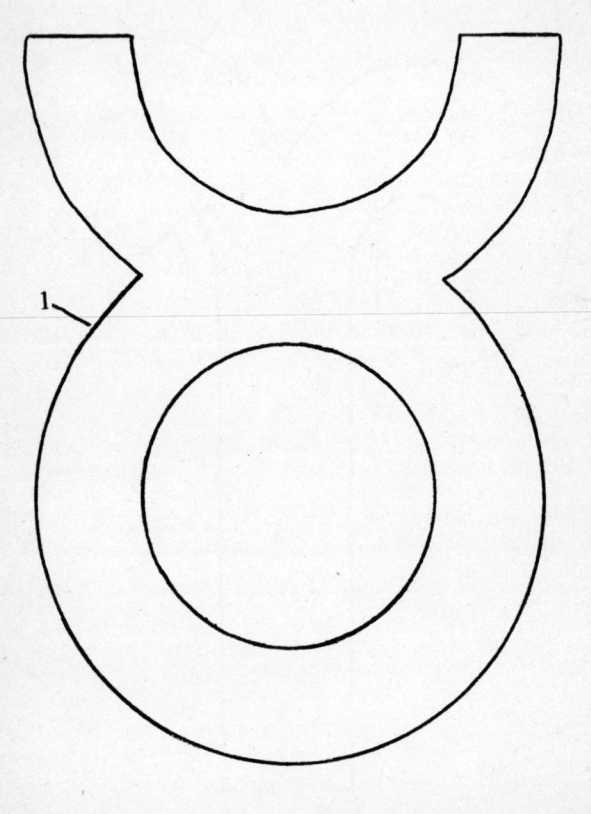

Figure 47f. Stitch Key for Taurus (April 20–May 21) Zodiac Sign: (1) Coral Knot Stitch.

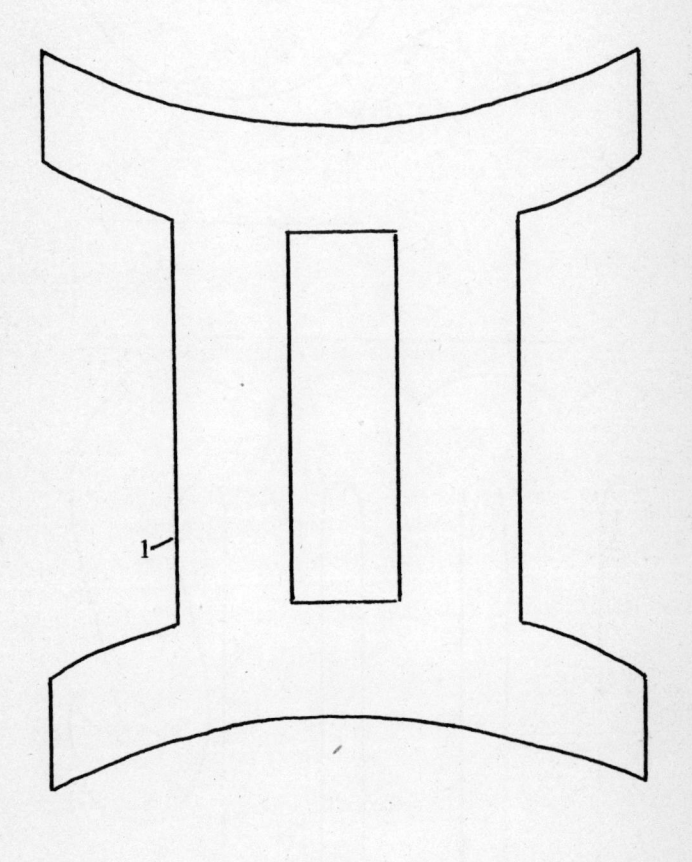

Figure 47g. Stitch Key for Gemini (May 21–June 21) Zodiac Sign: (1) Coral Knot Stitch.

74

75

Figure 47h. *(Opposite page, top.) Stitch Key for Cancer (June 21–July 23) Zodiac Sign: (1) Coral Knot Stitch.*

Figure 47i. *(Opposite page, bottom.) Stitch Key for Virgo (August 23–Sept. 23) Zodiac Sign: (1) Coral Knot Stitch.*

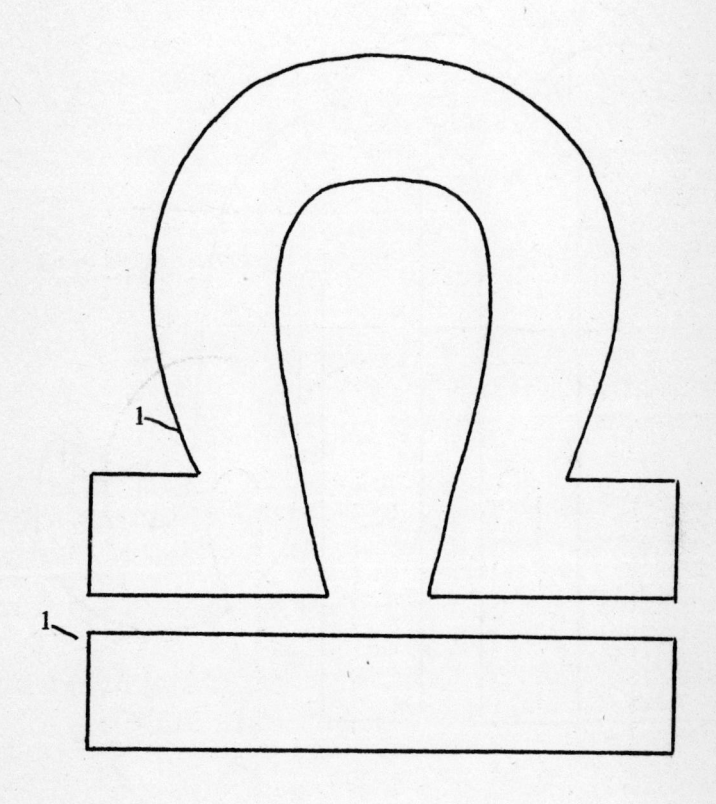

Figure 47j. Stitch Key for Libra (Sept. 23–Oct. 23) Zodiac Sign: (1) Coral Knot Stitch.

Figure 47k. Stitch Key for Scorpio (Oct. 23–Nov. 22) Zodiac Sign: (1) Coral Knot Stitch.

Figure 47l. Stitch key for Sagittarius (Nov. 22—Dec. 21) Zodiac Sign: (1) Coral Knot Stitch.

Top left: The Big Apple is a great motif and looks especially well on this short-sleeved sweatshirt (See page 80.)

Middle: All A-Flutter makes for an interesting design on this plain denim bag. (See page 83.)

Top right: Back Interest—This posy design will be especially effective when stitched on your back pocket. (See page 112.)

79

Top: Pleasantly Peasant—This lovely design makes a plain drawstring blouse truly unique. (See page 96.)

Bottom: Falling Leaves tumbling down a pair of slacks. (See page 108.)

HOW TO MAKE A ZODIAC PATCH *(figure 48):*

Use an 8 inch x 8 inch piece of firm, smooth, heavy (but not thick and bulky), background fabric. Many upholstery fabrics are perfect. For other fabrics, like denim, which become limp with repeated washings, use organdy as a backing.

Transfer zodiac sign to the center of the fabric square. Draw two concentric circles around the design. Make the outer circle five inches in diameter and the inner circle 4-3/4 inches. Insert fabric in a six-inch embroidery hoop. Work Buttonhole Stitch around the edge of the circle using the two drawn outlines as a guide for stitches (diagram I). Embroider zodiac design.

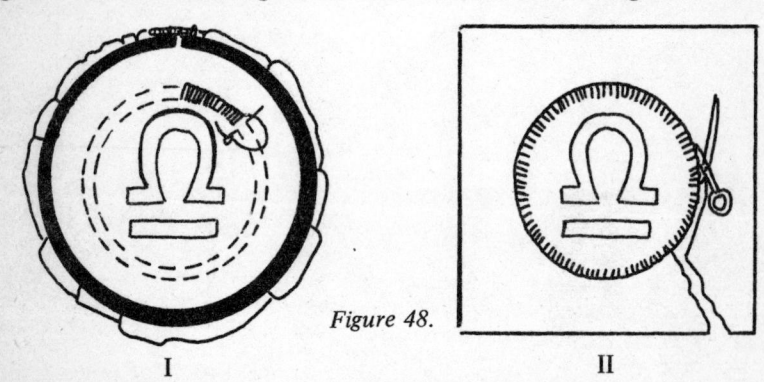

Figure 48.

I II

Remove piece from hoop and cut away excess fabric outside the buttonhole edge (diagram II). Clip close but don't cut the stitches. Apply patch to a garment with a white liquid clear drying glue, or sew patch in place. Many designs adapt well to a patch. And patches can be made in all sizes.

THE BIG APPLE *(figure 49):*

The big apple is a great motif that goes on sweat shirts, on jeans, on bibs, on hot pants, on and on, and on. . . .

Materials: One garment, your choice; knitting yarns (fabric will determine weight); tissue paper; a 6 inch x 6 inch piece of organdy for backing if design is to be put on a sweatshirt or other stretchy fabric.

Directions: Trace design on the tissue paper. Baste design on fabric as explained on page 23. Baste organdy backing material

Figure 49. Stitch Key for The Big Apple: (1) Stem stitch. (2) Straight stitch. (3) French knot. (4) Cross stitch.

to wrong side of fabric (applies only to stretchy backgrounds). Follow stitch key and embroider.)

82

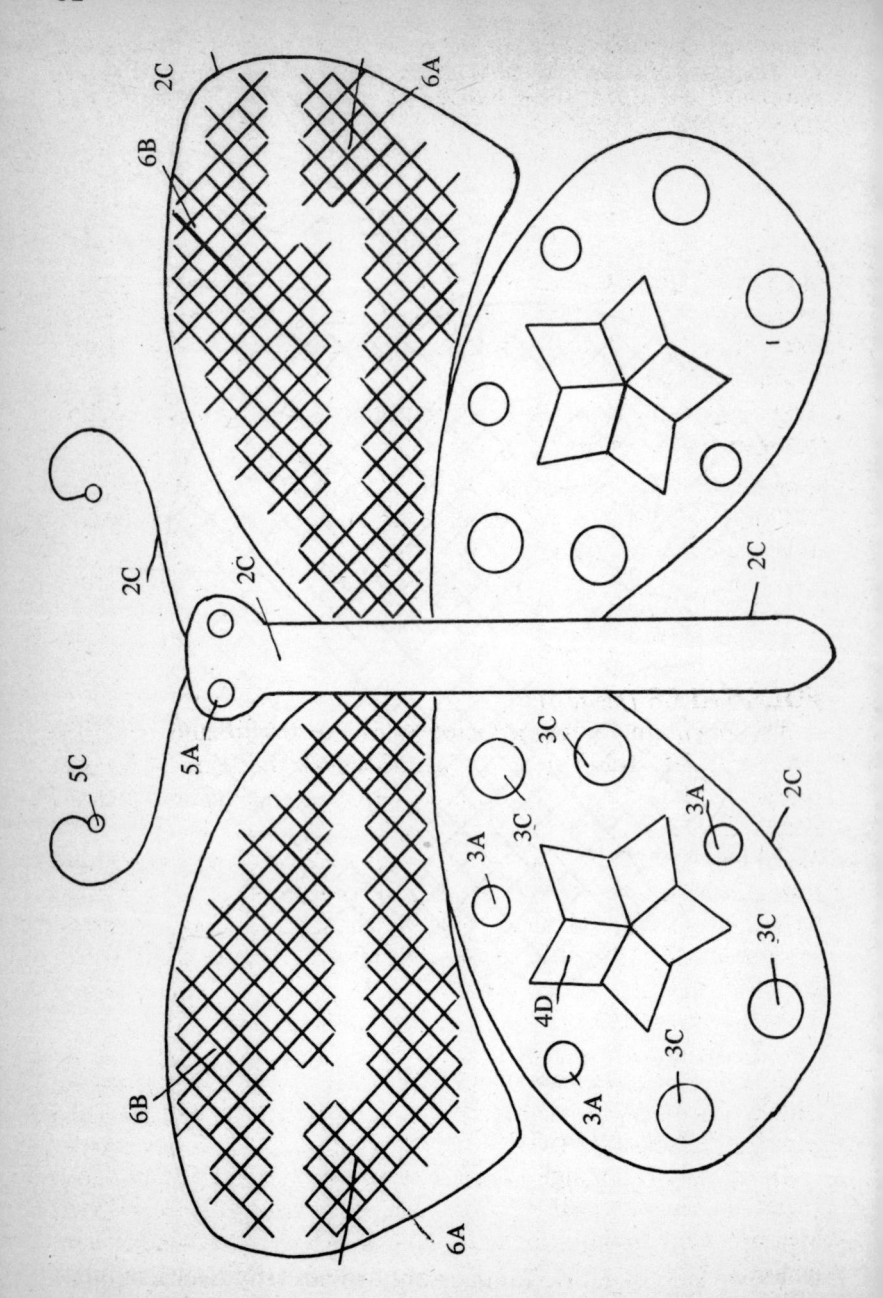

Figure 50. (Opposite page.) Stitch Key for All A-Flutter: (1) Chain stitch. (2) Chain stitch filling. (3) Satin stitch. (4) Fishbone stitch. (5) French knot. (6) Cross stitch. Color Key for All A-Flutter: (A) White. (B) Red. (C) Royal Blue. (D) Yellow.

ALL A-FLUTTER *(figure 50)*:

If you're all a-flutter about butterflies and red, white and blue turns you on, then this is the design for you. Try it on a denim bag or jacket.

Materials: Something denim; red, white, blue and bright yellow knitting worsted; tissue paper.

Directions: Trace pattern on tissue paper, then proceed as directed in tissue paper transfer method, page 23. Embroider following stitch and color key.

FOLK TALES *(figure 51)*:

The big item in peasant clothes is the bright and beautiful stitchery. It's traditional. Cross Stitch is traditional. So put them together. Cross stitch an easy-to-make traditional peasant skirt.

Materials: 2-½ to 3 yards of 45-inch wide linen or even-weave fabric (actual amount will depend on how full you wish skirt to be and your size. The above yardage should be enough for small to large size); 3/4-inch wide flat elastic long enough to fit around your waist; sewing thread to match fabric; 6-strand embroidery cotton.

Directions: Right sides facing, fold fabric in half crosswise. Stitch ¼-inch seam on the short edges. Stitch a 1-inch casing across one long side (waist), leaving an opening to insert elastic.

Draw elastic through casing. Overlap ends of elastic and sew them securely together. Sew casing closed. Try on skirt. Measure hem for midi or maxi length. Allow 3 inches for hem and cut off excess. Mark skirt with basting stitches where edge of hem will be. Don't hem skirt yet.

84

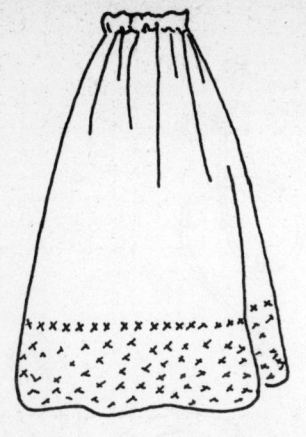

Figure 51. Folk Tales. (See chart on opposite page.)

Work Cross Stitch border just above line of basting stitches. This border is made by the thread count method (page 24). Start design at center back seam. Follow chart; each X on chart means one Cross on the fabric. Work each cross over 2 threads vertically and 2 threads horizontally. Repeat pattern around skirt.

Use 4 strands of embroidery cotton in the needle. Work design in one color. Next time try it in two colors.

When embroidery is finished, hem skirt.

For a wider border, repeat chart directly above first border.

ARTFUL ABSTRACT *(figures 52a and b):*

Come up abstract in vibrant shades or subtle tones. Whatever suits your mood. Transcend the ordinary. Plan your own design. Put it on a vest or tunic. Make it exclusively yours.

Materials: Purchased vest or tunic (solid color); knitting worsted in a color to match fabric; crewel or 3 ply yarns in assorted colors; sewing thread to match knitting worsted; crewel and sewing needle; tissue paper; pencil.

Directions: Use tissue paper to make a duplicate pattern of the right front of your vest or tunic. Now draw your own couching design on the pattern with pencil. Make it whatever you want it to be, but make it loose with lots of loops, curves and open spaces. Next, trace the flower motifs shown directly onto your

Figure 52a.

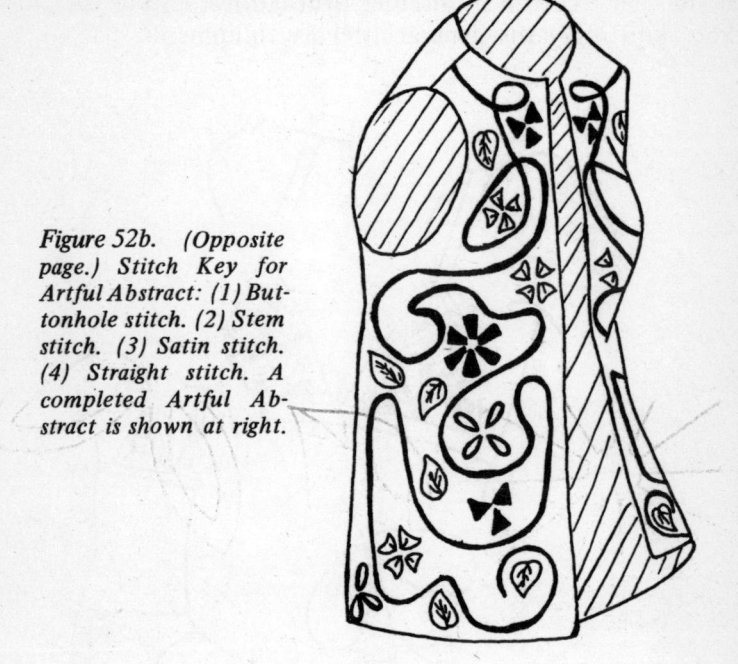

Figure 52b. (Opposite page.) Stitch Key for Artful Abstract: (1) Buttonhole stitch. (2) Stem stitch. (3) Satin stitch. (4) Straight stitch. A completed Artful Abstract is shown at right.

pattern. Put the flowers in the loops and open spaces. Scatter them around. Put them anywhere.

Use another sheet of tissue paper and trace the completed pattern—but reverse it for the left side of your vest.

Baste patterns to vest fronts. Use the running stitch method (see page 23) and transfer design to the fabric.

Couch a double strand of knitting worsted on your wild line design with sewing thread or 3 ply yarn. Use just a tiny tie down stitch for the couching. Embroider motifs as stitch key suggests, or let your imagination guide you.

BIKINI STITCHERY *(figure 53)*:

Your bikini shows off the best of you. So while the girl watchers watch, show them some of your stitchery talent.

Materials: Bikini or 2 piece bathing suit (avoid stretch or elastic materials, select cotton or another firm fabric); crewel yarn or synthetic knitting yarns; general stitchery equipment.

Figure 53. Stitch Key: (1) Satin stitch. (2) French knot. (3) Chain stitch.

Directions: Trace design and transfer it to the bikini top. Scatter the design at random placing it in different directions. Lay motifs fairly close. You want an all over repeat design; not a hit or miss one.

If desired, transfer one or two of the motifs to the pants' front. Put one or two on the back also. Then you'll look good in all directions.

Embroider design following stitch key.

ONE FLOWER *(figure 54):*

Wait until you see what a single flower motif does for a blouse and a whole lot of other things. Put one at each point of a collar. Work one around every button hole. Repeat them in a row around the sleeves, or in a row down the sleeves from shoulder to wrist. And if you are really ambitious, scatter this flower all over the front of a blouse. Magic!

Materials: Solid color blouse, your choice of style; 6-strand embroidery cotton; crewel needle and general embroidery equipment.

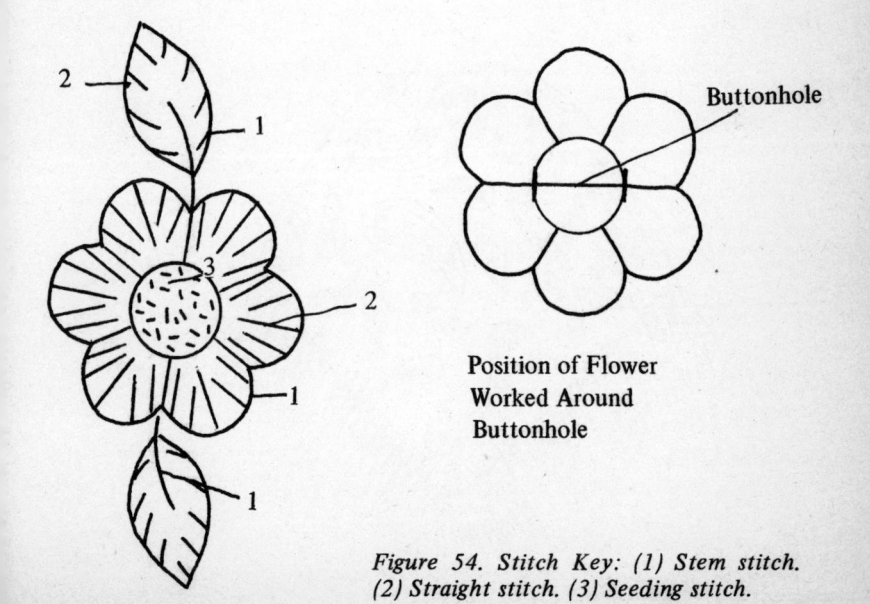

Position of Flower Worked Around Buttonhole

Figure 54. Stitch Key: (1) Stem stitch. (2) Straight stitch. (3) Seeding stitch.

Directions: Trace flower design and transfer to areas desired. Use 3 or 4 strands, depending on the blouse fabric, of the 6-strand embroidery cotton in the needle. Work design as stitch key suggests. When working flowers around buttonhole, work seeding stitch only where space allows. Enlarge design if needed to fit size of buttonhole.

YE OLDE PAISLEY SHAWL *(figures 55a – c):*

Make your shawl in a light weight wool fabric or a soft, light weight velour. And the design—it couldn't be more perfect. Everyone knows that paisley means shawl in Scotland.
Materials: 45-inch square of fabric; 4 ply knitting worsted (you will need several extra ounces for the fringe); crewel needle, tissue paper, piece of cardboard; crochet hook.

Directions: Be certain fabric is a true square cut on straight threads. If it isn't, you will have to sacrifice a few inches and cut raw edges on straight threads. Turn under ½-inch hems on all sides; baste them in place. Blanket Stitch all edges working stitches about ½-inch apart. Use yarn to match or contrast with the fabric.

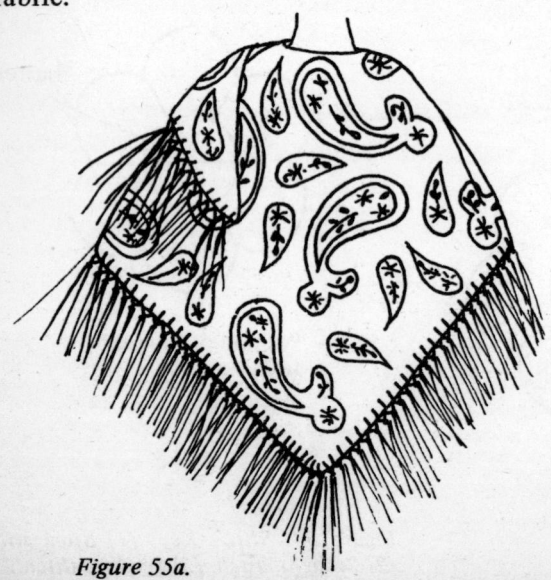

Figure 55a.

91

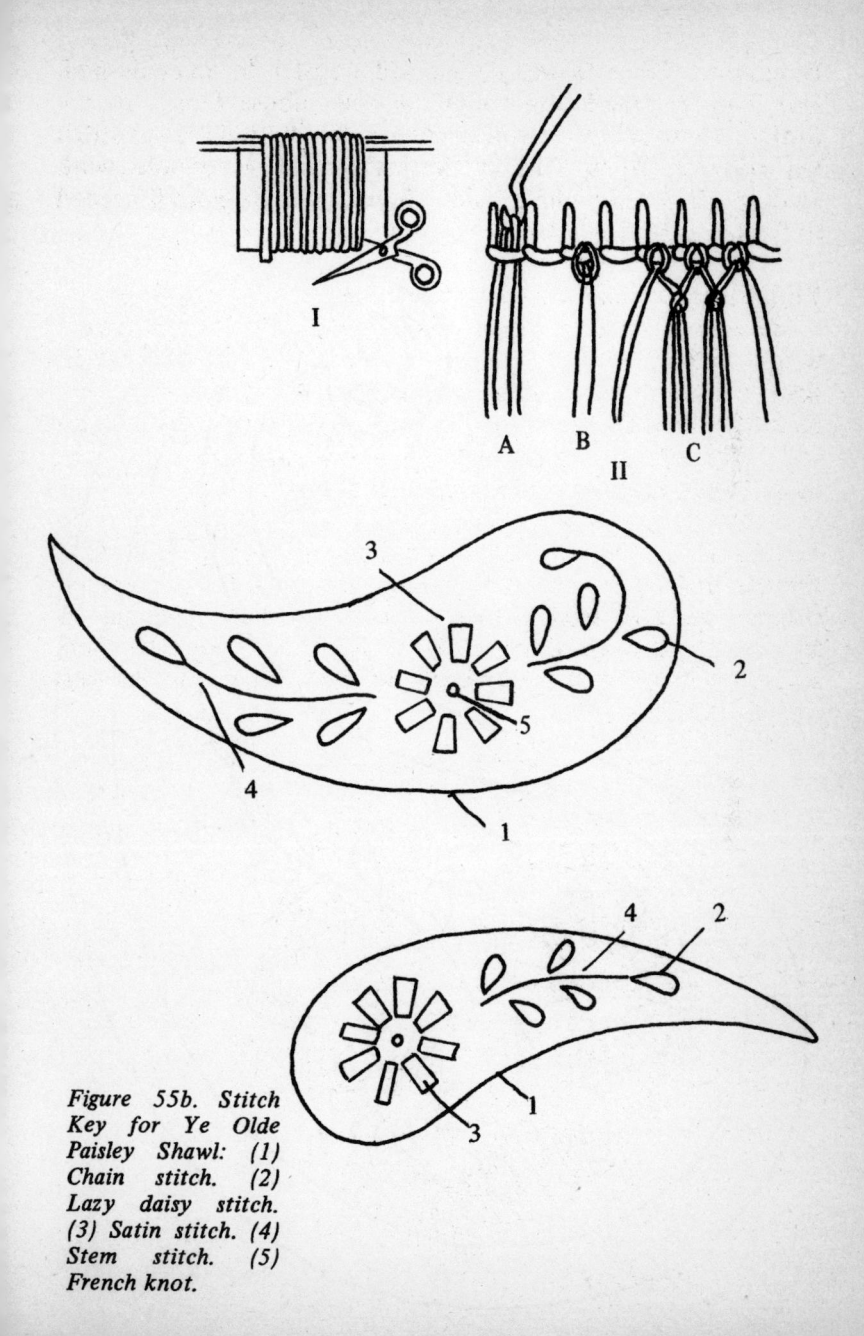

Figure 55b. Stitch Key for Ye Olde Paisley Shawl: (1) Chain stitch. (2) Lazy daisy stitch. (3) Satin stitch. (4) Stem stitch. (5) French knot.

92

Figure 55c. Stitch Key for Ye Old Paisley Shawl: (1) Chain stitch. (2) Lazy daisy stitch. (3) Satin stitch. (4) Stem stitch. (5) French knot.

To cut yarn for fringe, use a strip of cardboard 8 inches wide. This will make a fringe approximately 6 inches deep. Wrap yarn around cardboard, cut along one edge (diagram I).

To apply fringe to shawl, double two strands of cut yarn in half. Insert crochet hook in a blanket stitch and pull fold of strands through (diagram II-A), forming a loop. Pull ends of strands through loop to knot them (diagram II-B), to make a tassel. Repeat in each buttonhole stitch. When all tassels are complete, tie them to make a knotted fringe. Take two strands of one tassel and two strands of an adjacent tassel and knot them together (diagram II-C). Repeat all around.

Trace patterns onto tissue paper. If using one of the suggested materials, then you must use the tissue paper and running stitch method of transferring. Therefore you will need quite a few copies of the paisley designs (*figure 55c*).

Pin paper tracings on the shawl. Arrange and rearrange the paisleys until you have an all over well-balanced design. Baste tracings in place.

Embroider designs with stitches suggested in the stitch key using one strand of knitting worsted in the needle.

MATCH MATES *(figure 56, page 94)*:

Pair up your guy and you. Share a flower together. Or keep it all to yourself.

Materials: Unisex cotton or light weight shirts with breast pocket (one for you and one for him), or hot pants (for just you); 6-strand embroidery cotton, pencil and other usual stitchery equipment.

Directions: Trace half flower patterns. Transfer his flower to his shirt pocket. Put straight edge of flower along side edge of pocket (the side facing center front). With pencil, carefully and neatly write or print his name diagonally across the pocket. Keep pencil lines light. Now transfer your flower to your pocket and write your name.

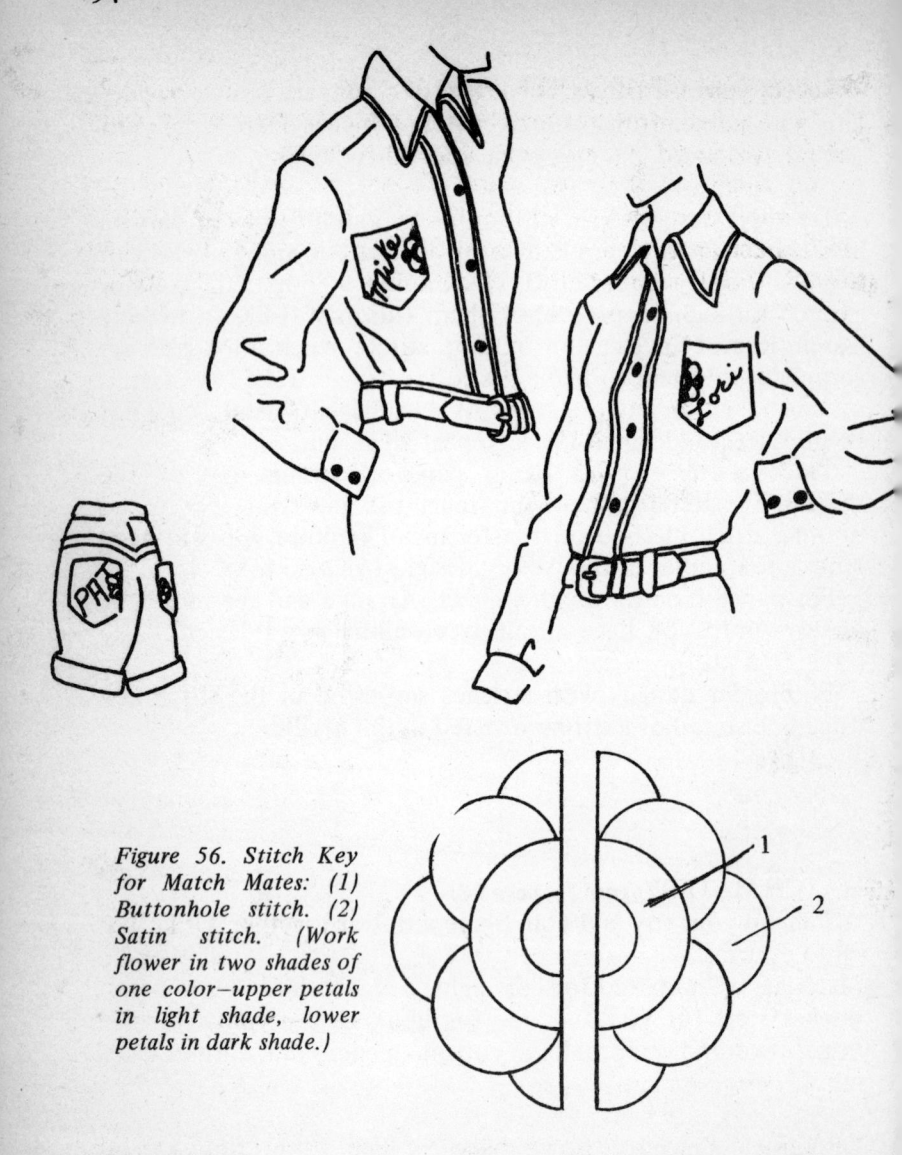

Figure 56. Stitch Key for Match Mates: (1) Buttonhole stitch. (2) Satin stitch. (Work flower in two shades of one color—upper petals in light shade, lower petals in dark shade.)

Using 4 strands of the 6 strand embroidery cotton, embroider name in stem stitch. Embroider flowers following stitch key using 3 strands of cotton in the needle.

For hot pants, put half a flower on each back pocket. Work names in 6 strands and flowers in 4 strands of cotton.

DRESS FOR GOOD TIMES *(figure 57):*

Let a stitch work for you. Let it create the design. The Tulip Stitch can do great things for a dress or a blouse.

To duplicate the dress panel shown, use a yard stick and pencil to lightly sketch straight lines for the panel. End panel 8 inches above hem edge. Embroider pencil line in Stem or Chain Stitch. Embroider another line outside but right next to the first line.

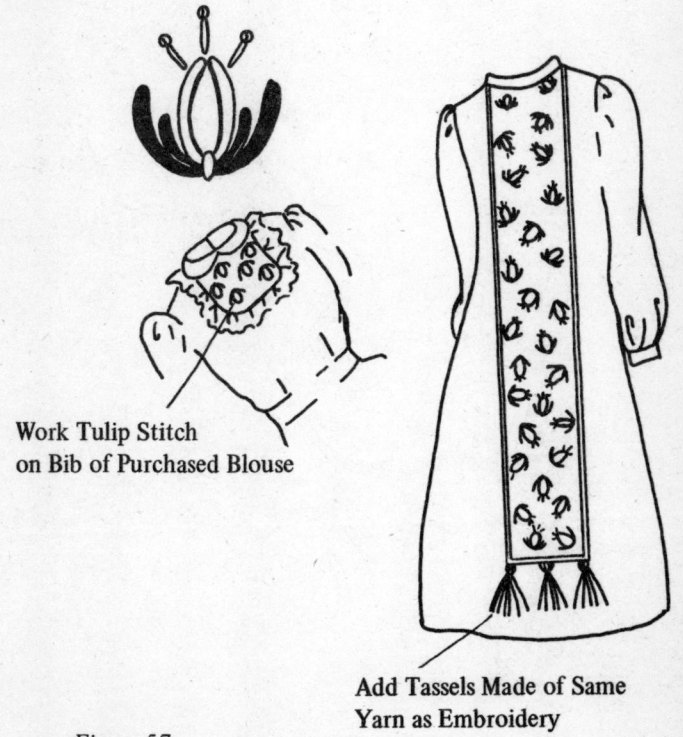

Work Tulip Stitch on Bib of Purchased Blouse

Add Tassels Made of Same Yarn as Embroidery

Figure 57.

Make a tissue paper pattern of the panel and plan the arrangement of the Tulip Stitch. Lay pattern on dress and sew a tiny stitch wherever flower is to be embroidered.

Make all Lazy Daisy part of stitch first using a flower color. Then work arms in green. Finally add yellow or orange stamens with French Knots on Stems.

96

Figure 58. (Opposite page.) Stitch Key for Pleasantly Peasant: (1) Stem stitch. (2) Satin stitch. (3) Lazy daisy stitch. (4) French knot. (5) Buttonhole stitch. (6) Chain stitch. (7) Seeding stitch. (8) Threaded backstitch (double) (two rows side by side) (9) Back stitch. (10) Fern stitch.

PLEASANTLY PEASANT *(figure 58):*

Be a pleasant peasant in a blouse that will be truly unique.
Materials: Purchased white, long sleeved, permanent press peasant blouse with drawstring neck (drawstring permits neckline opening to lie flat which makes the stitching easier); 6-strand embroidery cotton; large sheet of paper, ruler, pencil.
Directions: Enlarge or reduce pattern according to your needs. Trace pattern and transfer it to the left front side of blouse. Design should be placed along neck edge with top of design at shoulder and end of design at center front. Reverse design and transfer it to the right front of blouse.

Using 6 strands of embroidery cotton for large dots and 4 strands for small dots, embroider all French Knots. Work the rest of the design using 3 strands and following stitch key.

BABY'S BIB *(figure 59)*:

Another single flower and another great project. Now you can make any plain, back-fastened, dress or blouse the star attraction in your wardrobe.

Materials: Plain dress or blouse, with or without collar (back-fastened); embroidery cotton for light weight fabrics crewel yarn for medium and heavy weight fabrics; paper, pencil and ruler.

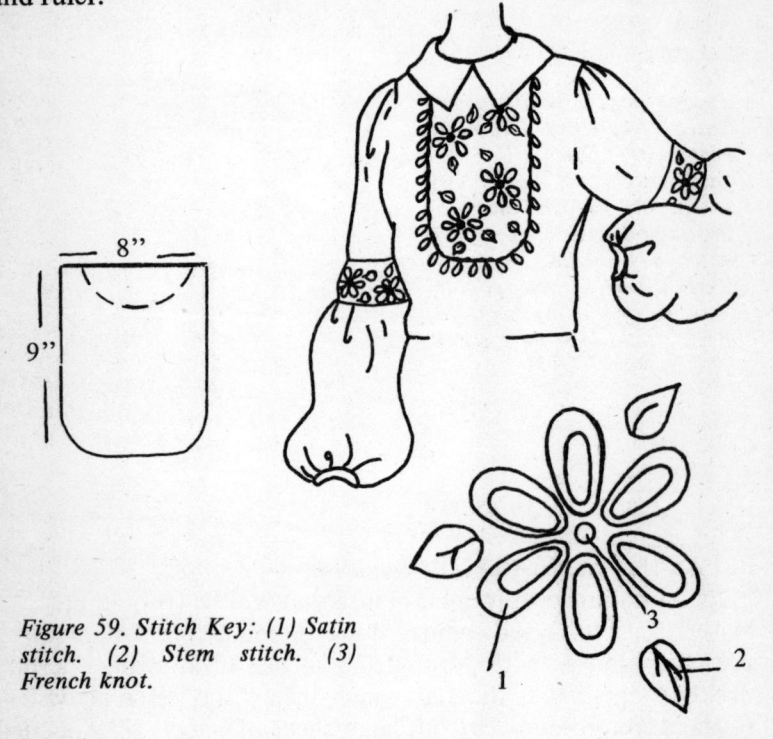

Figure 59. Stitch Key: (1) Satin stitch. (2) Stem stitch. (3) French knot.

Directions: On pager, draw a bib pattern about 9 inches long (or longer) and 8 inches wide. Cut curve for neckline. Try on bib; make any necessary adjustments.

Center bib pattern on front of garment; lightly trace around it with pencil. Embroider a row of Petal Stitch on the pencil line. Use 4 strands of embroidery cotton for light weight fabrics and 1 strand of crewel yarn for other fabrics.

Trace flower design and transfer to fabric. Scatter flower on bib inside petal stitching. Following stitch key, embroider flowers. Design may also be added to cuffs or bands around sleeves.

CIRCULAR DESIGNS *(figures 60a and b):*

The circle is an ideal shape for stitchery. Perfect for patches. Just use the basic circle shape to work stitches around, over and in. Add lines, dots and curves to that basic round shape and make circle designs.

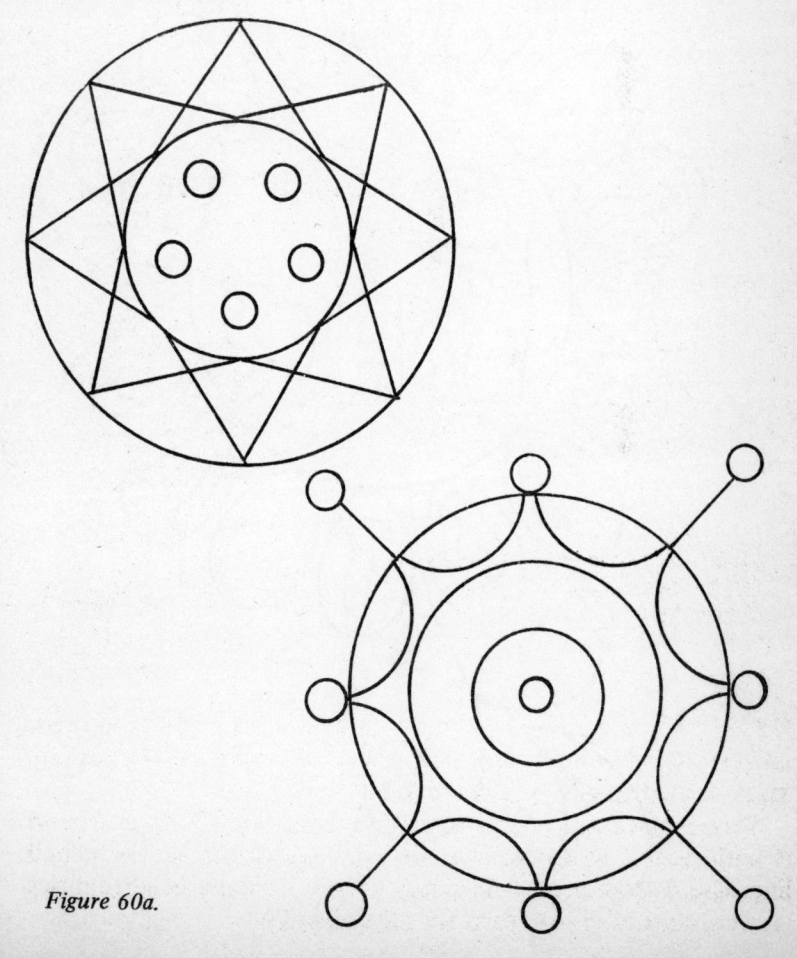

Figure 60a.

Figure 60b. Circular Designs.

All the following circular designs work up beautifully. Use them actual size or enlarge them. Put them wherever it suits you. Work them in your favorite stitches. Choose the yarns that make the most of the design.

PERKY PILLOW *(figures 61a and b):*
An easy circle design to toss around with stitchery. Create this design yourself and make it with quick stitches.
Materials: Two 14 x 14 inch squares of background fabric for pillow; knitting yarns (weight depends on background fabric), matching sewing threads; compass or jar lids in assorted sizes from 1 to 2 inches in diameter; pencil (black or light colored); two 14 X 14 inch squares of muslin; about one pound shredded foam rubber.

Directions: On one 14-inch background square, draw a 13½-inch in diameter circle *(figure 61a.)* Use a pot lid, large mixing bowl or something similar to trace around. Allowing for ½-inch seam, draw circles for flowers within the larger circle, using the jar lids to trace around. Don't make dark black pencil lines.

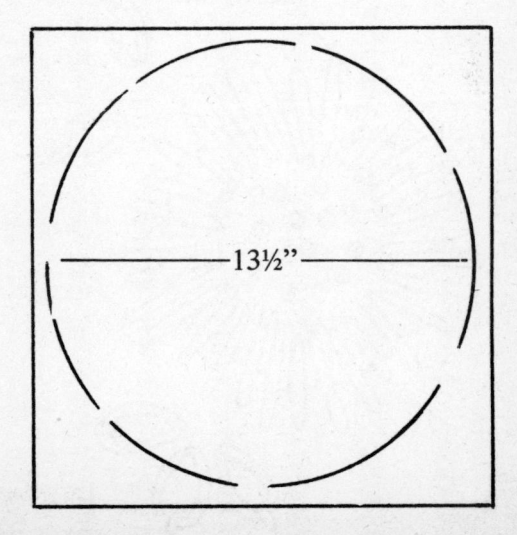

Figure 61a.

102

Figure 61b. Perky Pillow.

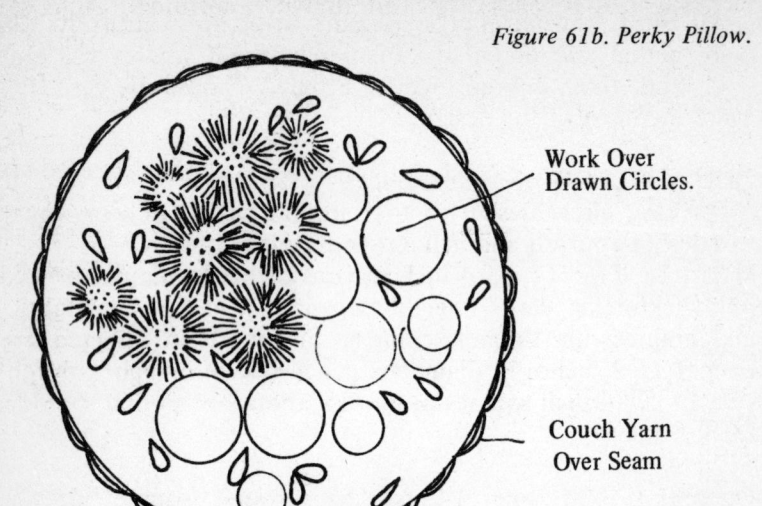

Work Over Drawn Circles.

Couch Yarn Over Seam

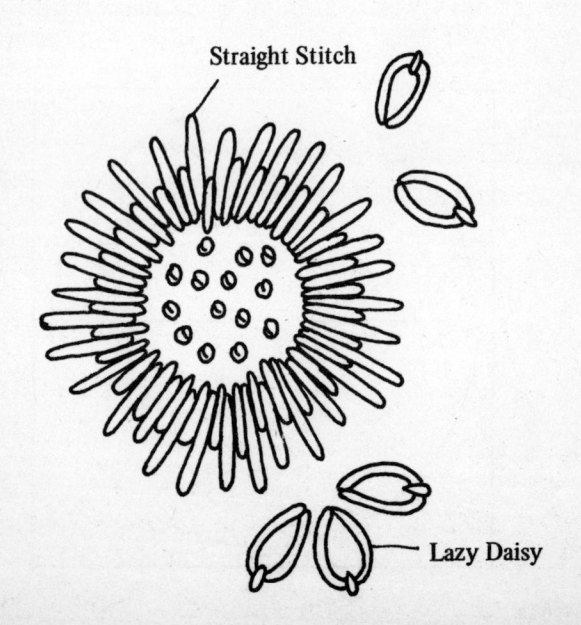

Straight Stitch

Lazy Daisy

When flower circles are all drawn, embroider each with Straight Stitches and French Knots as shown in figure 61b. Straight Stitches should vary in length and some flower centers should be off center or oval shaped so that all the flowers will not look exactly alike. Make some flowers in two shades of one color or two different colors using one shade for the inner short Straight Stitches and another for the outer long Straight Stitches. Keep stitches close together so that the perimeter of the circle is solidly covered. Vary the number and placement of the French Knots. Make Lazy Daisy leaves between and around the flowers wherever there is room.

Cut out the 13½-inch pillow circle. Draw and cut one for the back. Right sides facing, join front and back pieces together. Stitch around outside edge leaving an opening large enough for turning and inserting pillow form.

Make form from two 13½-inch in diameter muslin circles stitched together and firmly filled with shredded foam. Insert form in pillow cover; slip stitch opening closed.

Using four to six strands of yarn (depending on the weight of yarn used for stitchery), in the same colors used for the design. Couch around the pillow covering the seam.

DYNAMITE VEST *(figure 62):*

Figure 62.

An ideal gift for the man in your life. All this vest takes are satin stitched circles joined together to form an all over design of triangles. Make the triangles a variegated burst of color, or make each dot in the triangle a different shade of one color going from the lightest to the darkest. Like from baby blue (the color of his eyes?), to navy blue, with every shade of blue in between.

SWINGING HAMMOCK *(figure 63a – c):*

This hammock is a big project, but one that's well worth the effort. A truly individual piece that guests are sure to admire. Give it as a gift and you'll always be remembered.

Materials: Plain canvas hammock (available from Army-Navy Surplus stores); 4 ply knitting worsted in assorted colors; pencil; yardstick; compass or two jar lids, one 2-3/4 inches in diameter and one 3½ inches in diameter; piece of stiff cardboard.

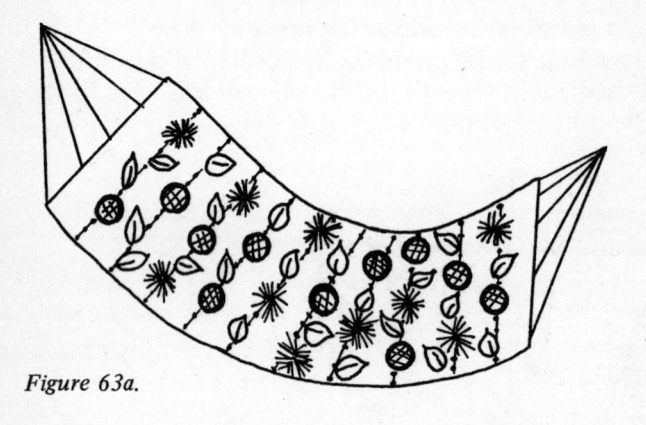

Figure 63a.

Directions: Lay hammock smoothly on a flat surface. With pencil and yardstick, draw lines about every 3 inches across width of hammock. Better measure length of hammock first to determine just how many inches from the top end you should start your first line. The last line you draw should be the same distance from the bottom end.

Using compass or the 3½ inch jar lid and *Figure 63b* for inspiration, place lid on hammock over penciled lines and trace

Figure 63b.

around it with pencil to make flower circles. Stagger flowers across hammock. Don't put them too close together.

Draw a 2-3/4-inch circle in the center of some of the drawn circles. Trace around it to make flower shapes like the ones shown above.

Trace pattern for leaf and transfer to stiff cardboard. Cut out and use leaf as a template. Lay leaf on hammock and trace around it. Scatter leaves at random wherever they fit and look best.

Using two strands of 4-ply knitting worsted in needle, embroider lines across hammock in Coral Knot Stitch. Do not embroider those sections of lines covered by flower and leaf designs.

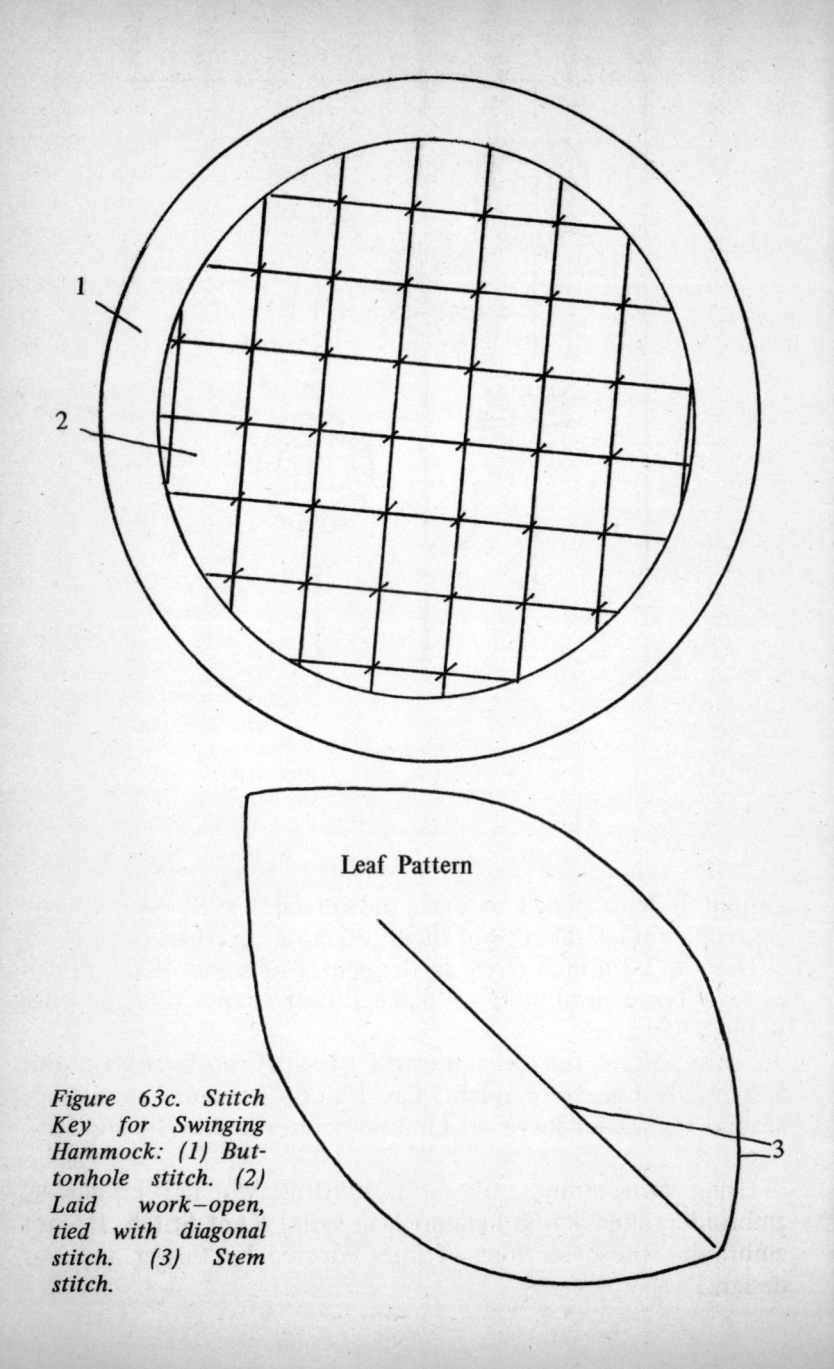

Figure 63c. Stitch Key for Swinging Hammock: (1) Buttonhole stitch. (2) Laid work—open, tied with diagonal stitch. (3) Stem stitch.

With one strand of knitting worsted, embroider single circles in Straight Stitches fanning out from the center of the circle (*figure 63b*). Following stitch key, embroider double circle flowers and leaves using a single strand of knitting worsted.

SUNNY FLOWER SEAT *(figures 64a and b):*

Put yourself in the director's chair! Sit down and stitch yourself a bunch of soft comfort.

Materials: Canvas director's chair (although it is possible to stitch directly on the canvas back and seat while they are attached to the chair frame, it is much easier to work on a replacement set. If possible, purchase replacement covers, stitch them, then put them on the frame. (Then apply stitchery to the original covers and have another set for a quick change.) You will also need crewel or 3-ply yarn, or 4-ply worsted if you prefer bulkier flowers; compass or 3½-inch in diameter jar lid and a pencil.

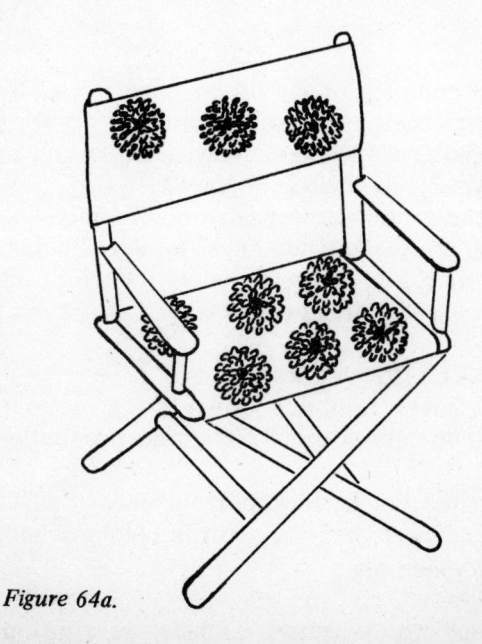

Figure 64a.

Figure 64b. Sunny Flower Seat.

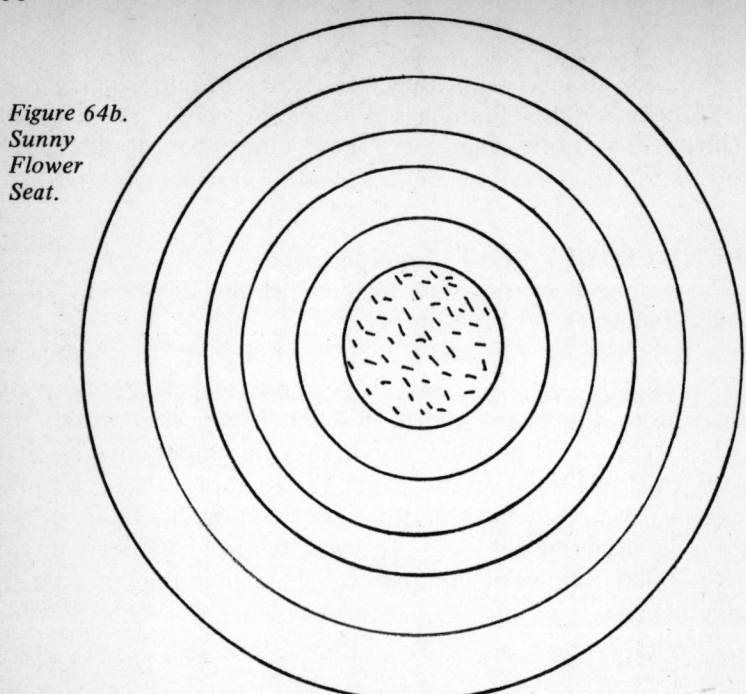

Directions: Use compass or jar lid to draw circles for flowers directly on canvas back and seat. Put circles wherever you want them; in any pattern you like. Now draw several concentric circles inside each 3½-inch circle as shown.

Except for the center, flower is worked completely in Petal Stitch. Starting on the outside ring, work each ring in order until all but center of circle is covered with Petal Stitches. Work Seeding Stitch in center of flower.

FALLING LEAVES *(figures 65a – c):*

Free falling leaves tumbling down a leg of your favorite pants. The stitches are a cinch. The end product speaks for itself.

Materials: Pants, cover-alls, flare bottom jeans or any other pair of plain slacks; crewel or 3-ply yarn in colors of your choice; embroidery paraphernalia.

Directions: Trace leaf patterns. Transfer to front pants' leg. Start at top of leg and arrange large leaves alternately with small

109

Figure 65a. Stitch Key for Falling Leaves: (1) Back stitch. (2) Chain stitch. (3) French knots.

*Figure 65b.
Falling Leaves,
another design.*

*Figure 65c.
Falling Leaves,
still a third
option.*

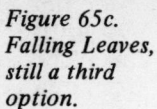

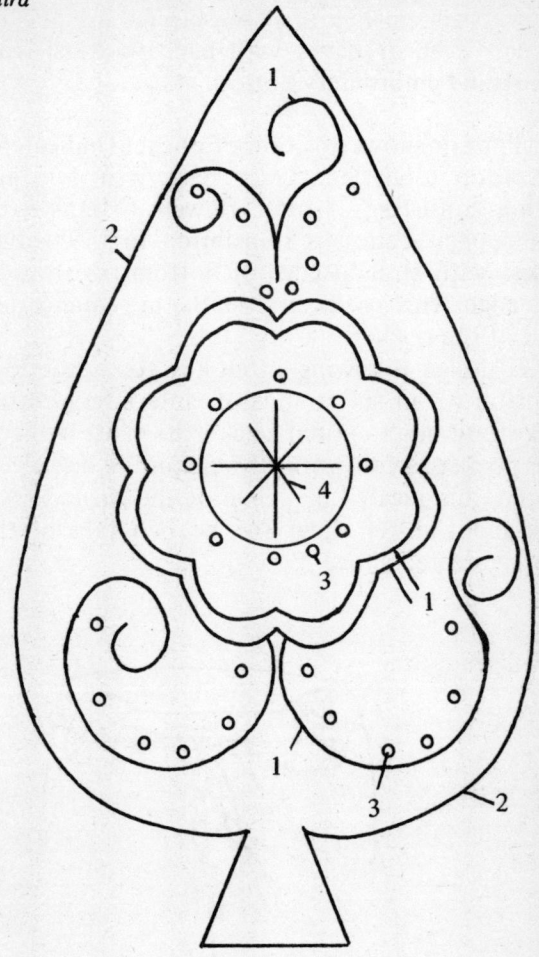

ones. Large leaves stand up, small leaves take off in any direction.

Embroider following stitch key.

BACK INTEREST *(figures 66a and b):*

From any point of view you're interesting. But wait until you walk away! You'll leave them applauding when you plant this posy design in your pocket. It's a sensational hip pocket design. Materials: Any pair of pants with back pockets; No. 5 pearl cotton or 6-strand embroidery cotton.

Directions: Pattern shows position of pocket (indicated by dash lines) in relation to design. Trace pattern in two parts. The lower portion consisting of three flowers is transferred to the pocket. The upper section is transferred to the pants directly above pocket with straight edge of bottom two flowers below the pocket edge. This position gives the appearance of flowers growing out of the pocket.

Embroider design following stitch key. Use either one strand of pearl cotton or all six strands of embroidery cotton in the needle. Take care not to stitch pocket to pants by keeping one hand inside pocket as you work flowers on the outside.

How about this idea? Take some of the single flowers from this design and transfer them to the belt tabs of the pants. Embroider as directed above.

Figure 66a.

Figure 66b. Stitch Key for Back Interest: (1) Satin stitch. (2) Stem stitch. (3) French knots. (4) Seeding.

114

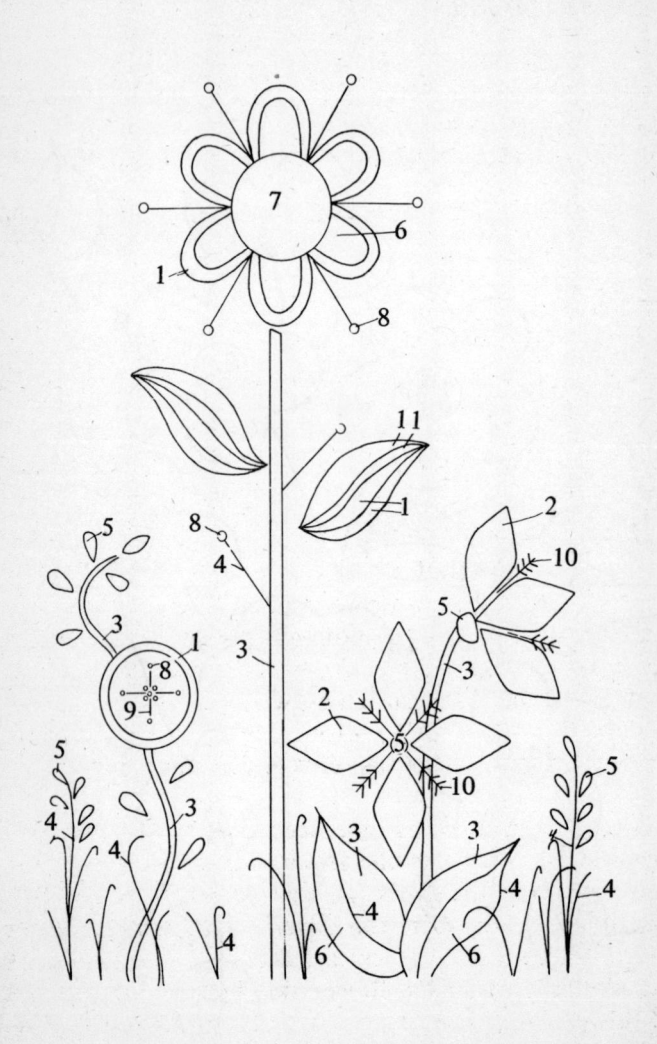

Figure 67. (Opposite page.) Stitch Key for In A Flower Garden: (1) Buttonhole stitch. (2) Fishbone. (3) Stem stitch filling. (4) Stem stitch. (5) Satin stitch. (6) Seeding stitch. (7) Laid work–open filling, tied with french knots. (8) Large french knots. (9) Straight stitch. (10) Fern stitch.

IN A FLOWER GARDEN *(figure 67)*:

Grow things! Make a flower garden. Pick just the right spot on the lower edge of bell bottoms. Plant stitches with tender loving care. Watch the stems grow, the leaves sprout, the flowers bloom. How does your garden grow?

Materials: Purchased bell bottom slacks; 3-ply or crewel yarns; large piece of paper (shelf paper is good); ruler; pencil.

Directions: Enlarge or reduce according to your needs. Trace design and transfer it to the lower edge of each pant leg. Place tallest flower on the front of leg just to the side of the side seam, about midway between the side seam and the center front crease. Repeat short flowers around pants alternating them so you don't have the same flower side by side. Do not repeat the large flower.

Following stitch key; embroider.

Another suggestion: plant this flower garden around the hem of a skirt, tunic or dress. A blooming success!

BORDER PRINT *(figure 68):*

Border print a classic dirndl with rows of double threaded Back Stitch and Chevron Stitch. Use a coarsely woven fabric with threads you can count and follow.

Construct skirt using directions given in Folk Tales project on page 83. Embroider using crewel or 3-ply yarns, or 6-strand embroidery cotton.

Figure 68.

117

KICKY KNICKERS *(figures 69a and b):*

Be a most fashionable urchin. Stitch a couple of patches on your knickers, slip on a pair of knee-high snug boots and you're ready for action.

Materials: Purchased knickers, crewel or knitting yarns (weight depends on background fabric).

Directions: Trace designs for patches. Transfer to knee or seat of knickers, or both. Following stitch key, embroider patches in a variety of bright colors.

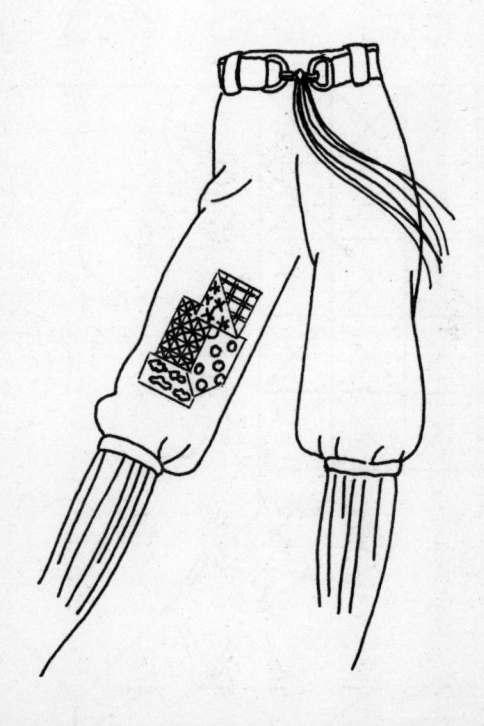

Figure 69a. Kicky Knickers.

118

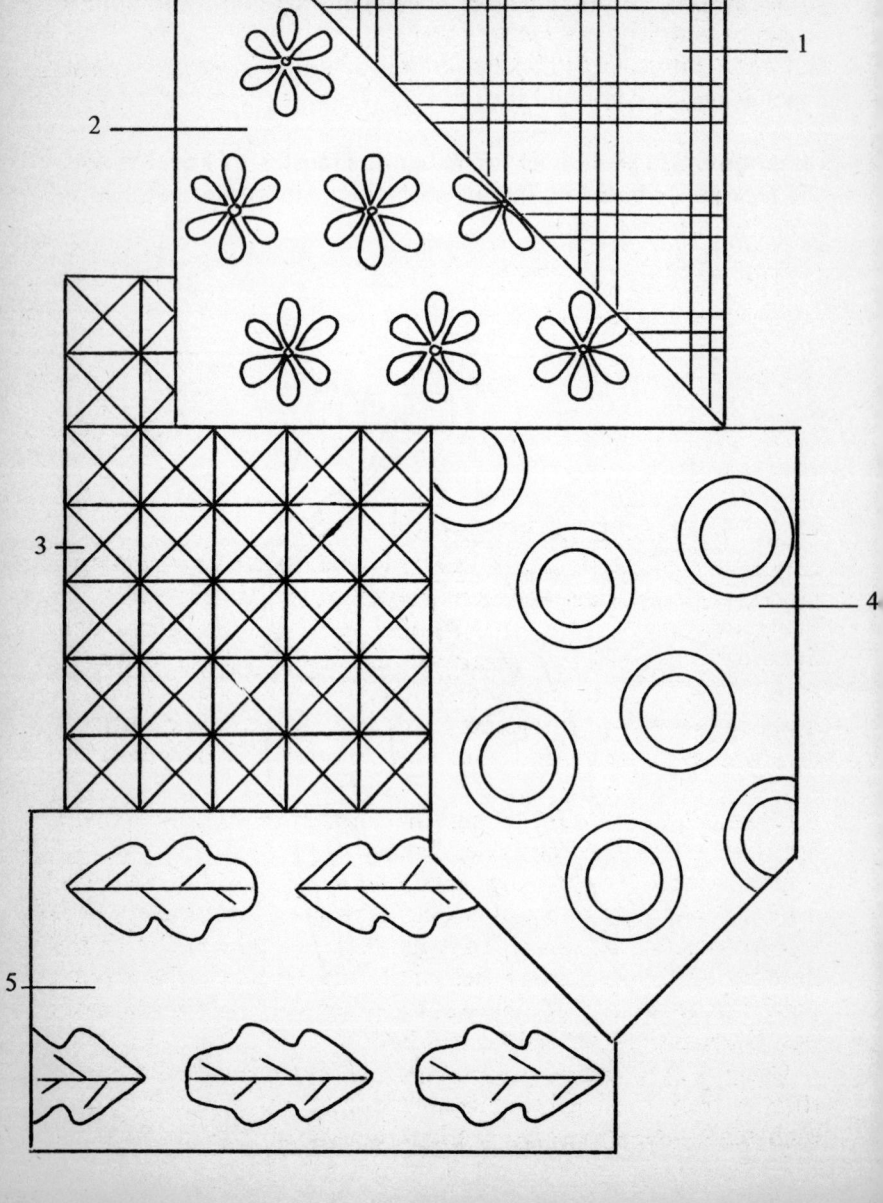

Figure 69b. Stitch Key for Kicky Knickers patches on opposite page: Patch 1: Use split stitch for all lines. Work horizontal lines in one color, then vertical lines in another color. Patch 2: Lazy daisy flowers, french knot centers. Patch 3: Work horizontal lines, then vertical lines in stem stitch. Make cross stitch in each block. Patch 4: Work all rings in buttonhole stitch. Patch 5: Work all leaves in back stitch.

Another suggestion: Try patched elbows on a denim jacket or wool blazer.

PATCHWORK TIE SKIRT *(figure 70)*:

A bunch of men's ties, a variety of stitches and you'll have a patchwork skirt that's different but definitely in fashion.

Materials: Men's ties, the amount depends on your size; however, be unique in your choice of material, i.e. use all cotton, all silk or all wool—otherwise cleaning will be a problem; 6-strand embroidery cotton; 3/4-inch wide elastic, long enough to fit around your waist; lining fabric if desired.

Directions: Remove stitching that holds back seam of ties together. Unfold and press ties flat.

With narrow ends at top, take one tie and lay the side edge over the side edge of another tie. Edges should overlap about ¼ inch. Baste ties together. Take another tie and baste it to the first tie. Continue adding ties until your tie fabric fits around your hips with ease. If you want a fuller skirt, add a few more ties. Overlap first and last tie and baste.

Using 4 or 6 strands of embroidery cotton in needle, select stitches from the suggested list and work a row of stitching over each seam where one tie overlaps the other. Use a variety of

120

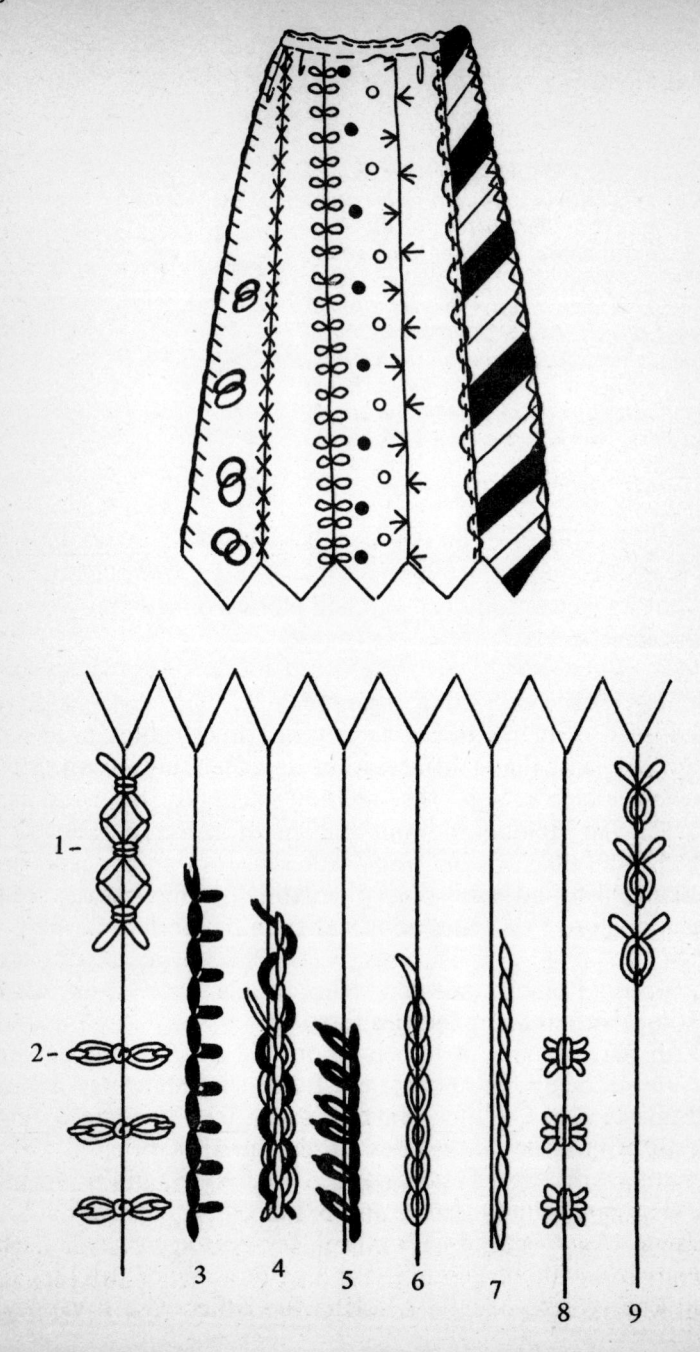

Figure 70. (Opposite page.) Suggested stitches for Patchwork Tie Skirt: (1) Fly stitched crossed. (2) Lazy daisy stitch bows, french knot centers. (3) blanket stitch. (4) Back stitch—double threaded. (5) Petal stitch. (6) Chain stitch. (7) Stem stitch. (8) Sheaf stitch. (9) Wheat ear stitch.

Also Try: Pekingnese stitch, coral knot stitch, closed button hole stitch, fern stitch, cross stitch.

stitches, a different one for each seam. Be sure to stitch through all thicknesses of fabric because the embroidery is what holds the skirt together.

When embroidery is complete, decide on length you want skirt; add 2 inches for casing. Measure skirt from the pointed hem edge (the wide end of ties) and cut off excess fabric at top of skirt. Be sure to cut straight.

If you want to line the skirt, use a light weight lining fabric. Cut lining the same size as skirt plus 1 inch for back seam (½-inch seam allowance). Sew back seam. Put lining inside skirt with wrong sides facing. Pin top edges of lining and skirt together; treat as though they were one fabric. Fold over 2 inches at top of skirt. Turn under ½ inch hem to make a 1½-inch casing. Top stitch close to top folded edge. Draw elastic through opening in casing. Overlap and sew ends of elastic securely together. Sew opening in casing closed. Hem lining just above pointed skirt edge.

CLINGING VINE *(figures 71a and b)*:

The clinging vine design grows on you. Plant it on the hem of your favorite pants where it will grow up the side seam. Plant it on a belt and it will encircle your waist easily.

Materials: For slacks you will need knitting yarns, weight depending on the background fabric. For belt you will need about ¼ yard of canvas or burlap; grosgrain or other firm ribbon

Figure 71a.
Clinging Vine

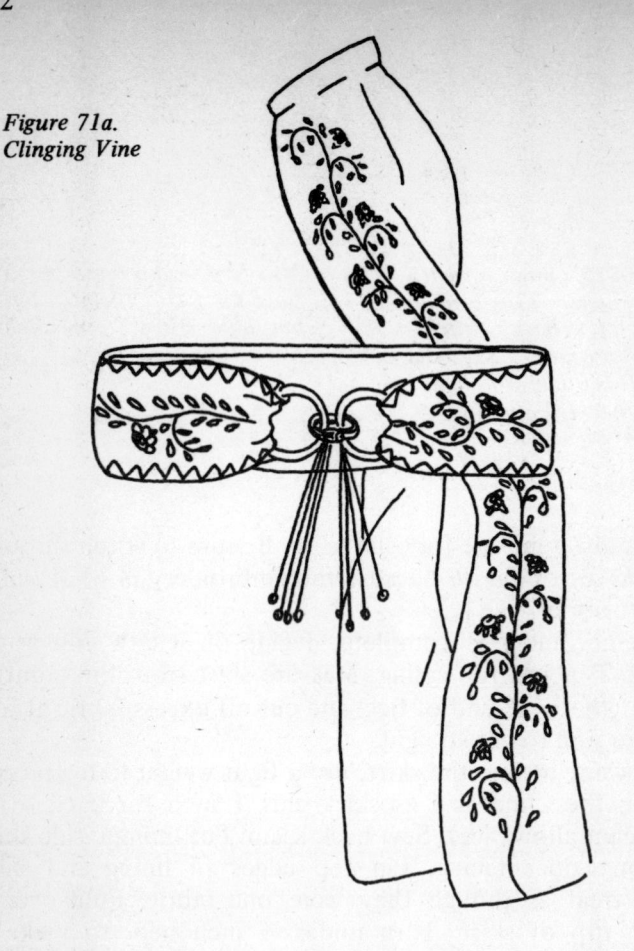

3 inches wide and as long as your waist measurement; two 2-inch brass plated rings.

Directions: For pants, use transfer method which best fits fabric. Repeat vine design for length required. Flowers are alternately placed from one side to the other along the vine. Transfer design to each outside seam so that it runs from bottom of leg to waist. Follow stitch key and embroider in desired colors.

Figure 71b. Stitch Key for Clinging Vine: (1) Chain Stitch. (2) Split stitch. (3) Satin stitch. (4) Lazy daisy stitch.

For Belt: First tape all raw edges of fabric with masking tape. Using either a basting stitch or a pencil, draw outline of belt 6½ inches wide two inches longer than waist measurement. The finished belt will measure 4½ inches wide, the extra 2 inches in width and length is seam allowance. Be sure to draw outline on straight fabric threads. Do not cut belt yet.

Center vine design on belt allowing 1 inch all around for the seam allowance. Embroider design following stitch key.

Cut out belt on drawn outline. Turn back seam allowances so that belt measures 4½ inches wide and the length of your waist. Baste seam allowance. Line belt with ribbon; slip stitch ribbon to back of belt turning under raw edges at each narrow end.

Work Closed Buttonhole Stitch along the top and bottom belt edges. Slip one end of belt through a brass ring. Turn end to inside of belt and sew securely in place. Attach other ring to the other belt end.

To tie belt, use several yarn strands in a combination of colors used for the stitchery. Cut strands as long as desired. Knot each end; lace strands through rings and tie together.

Next time you work this design, omit the Lazy Daisy leaves. Work the stem in Fern Stitch. It's different.

THE VERSATILE BAND *(figures 72a and b)*:

Headband, guitar strap, choker or belt, a whole battery of things can be made with this western motif. Run it around a skirt, up pants legs, down sleeves and over your shoulder on suspender straps.

For start-from-scratch projects—belts, headbands, guitar straps, chokers—start with a linen-like or light weight upholstery fabric. Cut a strip of fabric slightly wider than shown on pattern and as long as needed. Headband, choker and belt are all made the same way. Work stitchery, baste ½-inch seams and line with 1-3/4 inch wide firm ribbon (diagram I). Sew several yarn strands to each end of band for tying. Attach tassels if desired. For guitar strap, make it in the same way but use strap findings salvaged from an old guitar strap, or purchase hooks from shops selling makings for leather belts and bags, to attach strap to guitar.

For skirts, sleeves and pants, trace design and transfer directly to background fabric. Embroider following stitch key.

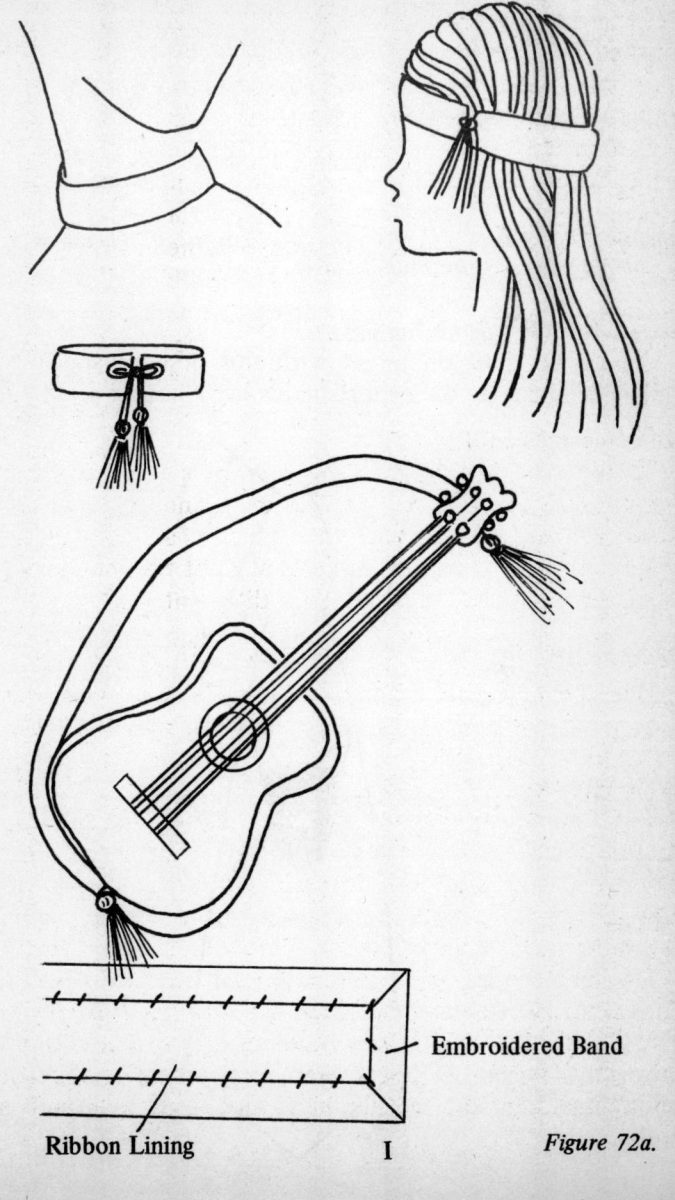

Embroidered Band

Ribbon Lining

Figure 72a.

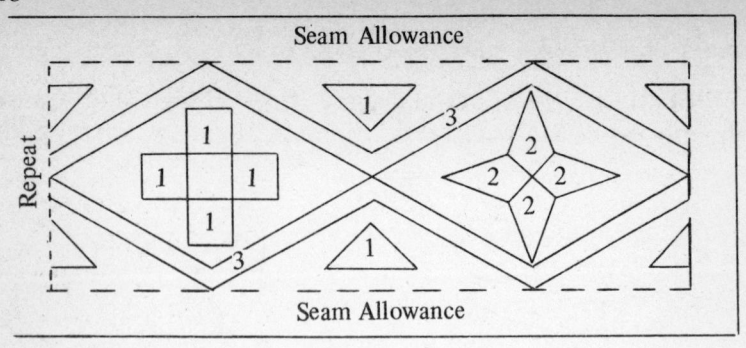

Figure 72b. Stitch Key for The Versatile Band: (1) Satin stitch. (2) Fishbone stitch. (3) Buttonhole stitch.

BULL'S EYE *(figures 73a and b)*:

You'll be right on target with this design, especially if you put it dead center on a sportsman's tie. Another great spot? The

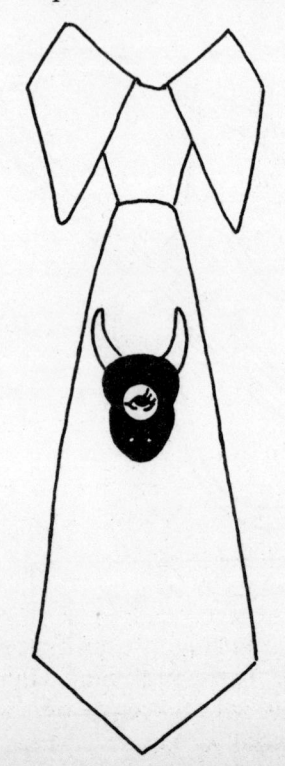

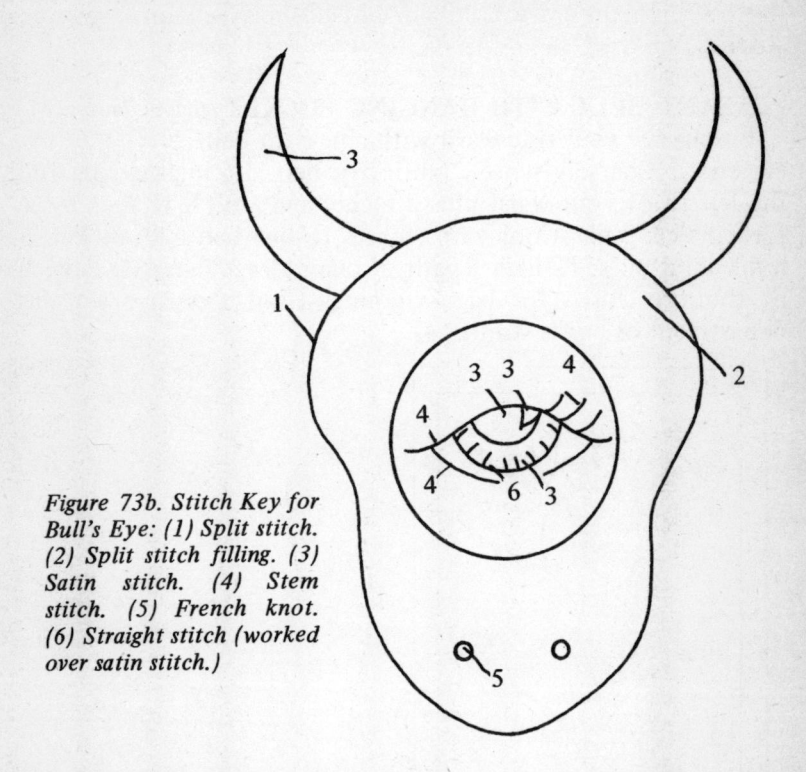

Figure 73b. Stitch Key for Bull's Eye: (1) Split stitch. (2) Split stitch filling. (3) Satin stitch. (4) Stem stitch. (5) French knot. (6) Straight stitch (worked over satin stitch.)

back pocket of jeans or hot pants.
Materials: Solid colored 4 or 5 inch wide tie; yarns compatible with the background fabric. (Why not make the complete tie? There are many easy patterns available.)

Directions: If you are making the tie from scratch, transfer design to fabric before cutting out tie. Trace outline of front tie pattern on fabric so that you'll put bull's eye dead center. Stitch design, then cut out and make tie. An all wool tie looks great worked in fine wool yarns.

When working on a purchased tie, take care not to pull it out of shape. Disregard all rules about working needle straight up and down through the fabric. Work stitches as for sewing taking them through front of tie only and not completely through to the back. Do not pull stitches tight. Follow key for suggested stitches.

PEASANT BELT WITH HANGING POCKET *(figures 74a and b)*.

Emphasize your tiny waist with a peasant belt.

Materials: Coarsely woven fabric for belt, 5½ inches wide and the length of your waist plus 2 inches and an 8 X 16 inch piece for pocket; 3-ply wool yarn; fabric to line belt and pocket; 3 hooks and eyes; 12 inch length of chain; large fancy hook such as the type used for bag fastenings (find this in a notions department or crafts store).

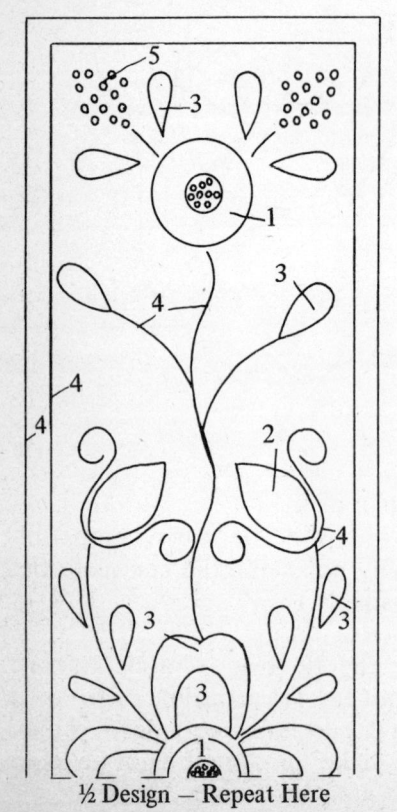

Figure 74a. Stitch Key for Belt with Hanging Pocket: (1) Buttonhole stitch. (2) Fishbone stitch. (3) Satin stitch. (4) Chain stitch. (5) French knots.

Belt Design

Figure 74b. Pocket Design.

Directions: Bind all edges of fabric with masking tape to prevent fraying. Trace and complete the half-design shown. Transfer design to fabric. Use design as you wish on your belt. Work it once on the center back of the belt or repeat it evenly spaced along the full length. Following stitch key, embroider design.

When stitchery is complete, fold 1-inch seam allowance to wrong side. Miter corners and baste hems in place. Cut lining fabric same size as belt, turn under ½-inch hems and slip stitch lining to belt.

Trace pocket design. Fold pocket fabric in half crosswise and center design correctly. Open fabric flat and embroider design.

Fold pocket in half crosswise, wrong sides facing. Machine or handstitch side seams ½ inch from edge. Turn pocket to right side and fold in top edge about 1½ inches. Cut lining same size as pocket, sew side seams. Slip lining inside pocket, wrong sides facing and fold down top hem. Slip stitch lining to pocket along top edge.

Sew the 3 hooks and eyes evenly spaced to front edge of belt. To attach pocket to belt, sew ends of chain to pocket corners. (A good substitute for chain is two heavy chain bracelets linked together.) Sew large belt hook to bottom edge of belt front, midway between center front and left side. Hang center link of chain on the belt hook. (If hook is unavilable, sew center link of chain to inside bottom edge of belt.)

NIFTY KNEE SOCKS *(figures 75a and b)*:

You're special, so why shouldn't everything about you be special from the top of your head to the bottom of your knee socks. Two different designs and two different placements add up to a pair of show-off legs.

Materials: Two pair purchased wool or acrylic knee socks; crewel or 3-ply yarn; general stitchery equipment.

Directions: Do not use a hoop for stitchery. Watch your tension. Don't pull stitches tight. Use transfer method for hand and machine knits.

Rose: Placing rose at top of sock; stem running to the foot, trace rose pattern and transfer to one side of each sock. Be sure

Figure 75a. Stitch Key for Nifty Knee Socks: (1) Satin stitch.

to put design on the outside leg or you'll end up with two alike and not a pair. Repeat stem for correct length. See stitch key for suggested stitches.

Primitive Design: Trace and transfer to sock just above ankle. Embroider following stitch key.

Figure 75b. Stitch Key for Nifty Knee Socks: (1) Satin stitch. (2) Stem stitch.

THINK THIRTIES *(figure 76)*:

Go with a skinny cap or beret. Wrap up in a long, long scarf. Head things and neck things are terrific for stitchery.

Materials: Purchased bulky knit cap and scarf set in solid color (must be solidly knitted, not open mesh type); 3- or 4-ply yarns.

Directions: Trace medallion design three times on tissue paper. Baste one tissue paper tracing to side of skinny cap or beret. Baste a tracing on each end of scarf. Embroider medallion following stitch key.

Figure 76. Stitch Key for Think Thirties: (1) Laid work—open. (2) Split stitch. (3) French knot. (4) Buttonhole stitch.

PEASANT PANEL *(figures 77a – c)*:

Join the peasant movement! Make this belted apron panel and you're in!

Materials: For midi length you will need linen or homespun type fabric, one piece 10½ inches wide and about 30 inches long for panel (or measurement from your waist to bottom of skirt hem plus 1 inch), and one piece 9 inches wide, long enough to fit your waist plus 1 inch for seams. You will also need crewel or 3-ply yarns; 3 hooks and eyes and sewing thread to match fabric.

Directions: Turn under a 1 inch hem on both sides and bottom edges of panel. Hand stitch with invisible stitches.

Trace border pattern. It is made in two sections. Connect section two to section one where indicated by dash lines. Repeat side border for length needed. Place tracing on one side of apron panel matching center front of design with center front of panel. Transfer design to background fabric. Reverse design and transfer it to the other side of apron. Embroider following stitch key.

Fold waistband in half lengthwise. Allowing ½ inch seam allowance, transfer waistband design to center front. Open waistband flat and embroider design.

Right sides facing; fold waistband in half lengthwise; stitch short ends making ½ inch seams. Turn to right side and fold in ½ inch hems along bottom edge. Insert top of apron panel in waistband matching center fronts; top stitch. Sew hooks and eyes to waistband edges.

More suggestions: Last year's plain shift can be in fashion this year. Embroider border design on front bodice and along sleeve edges or wrist band. Belt dress with drapery cord. Work border around the bottom of a tunic, flare bottom pants or on suspender straps.

134

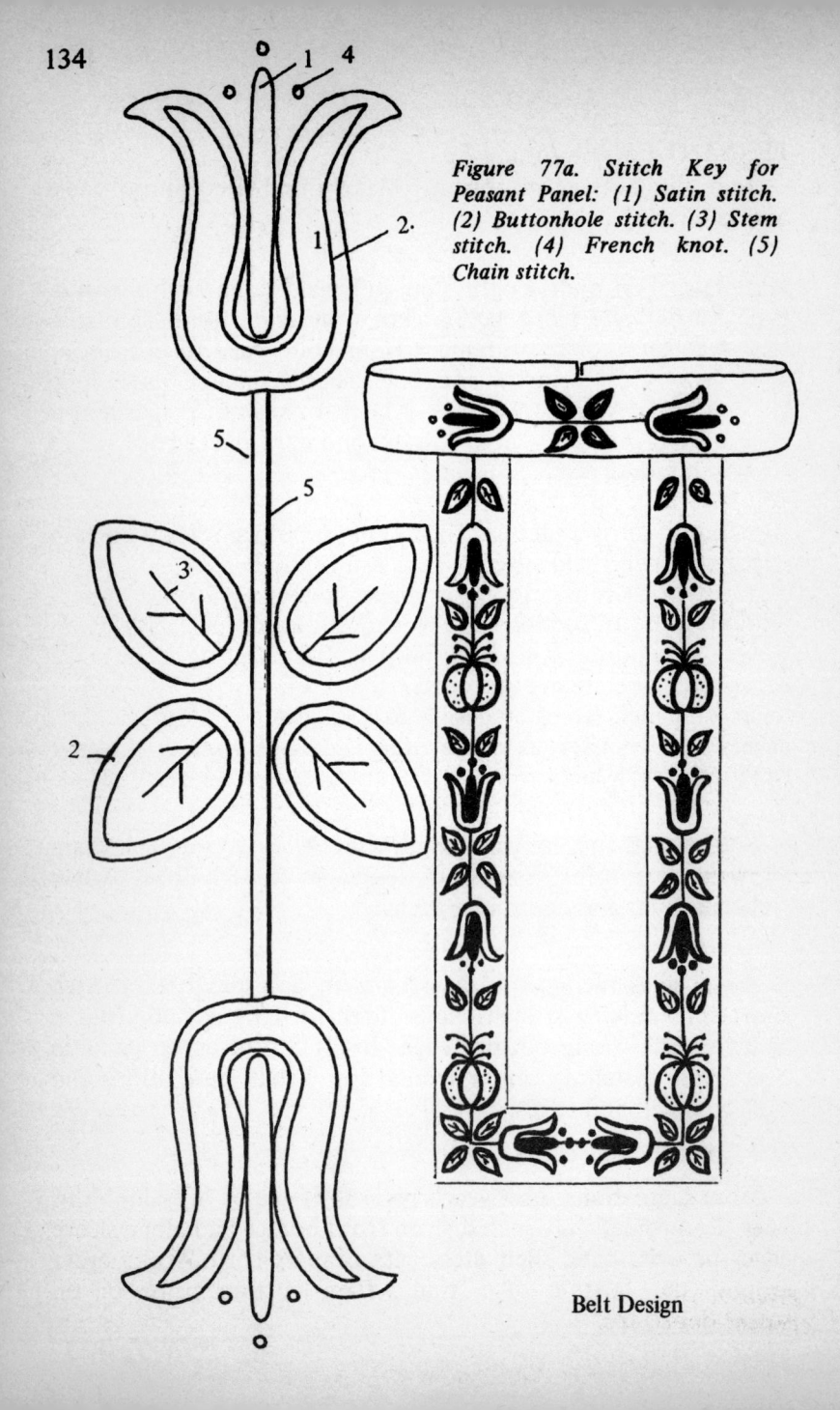

Figure 77a. Stitch Key for Peasant Panel: (1) Satin stitch. (2) Buttonhole stitch. (3) Stem stitch. (4) French knot. (5) Chain stitch.

Belt Design

135

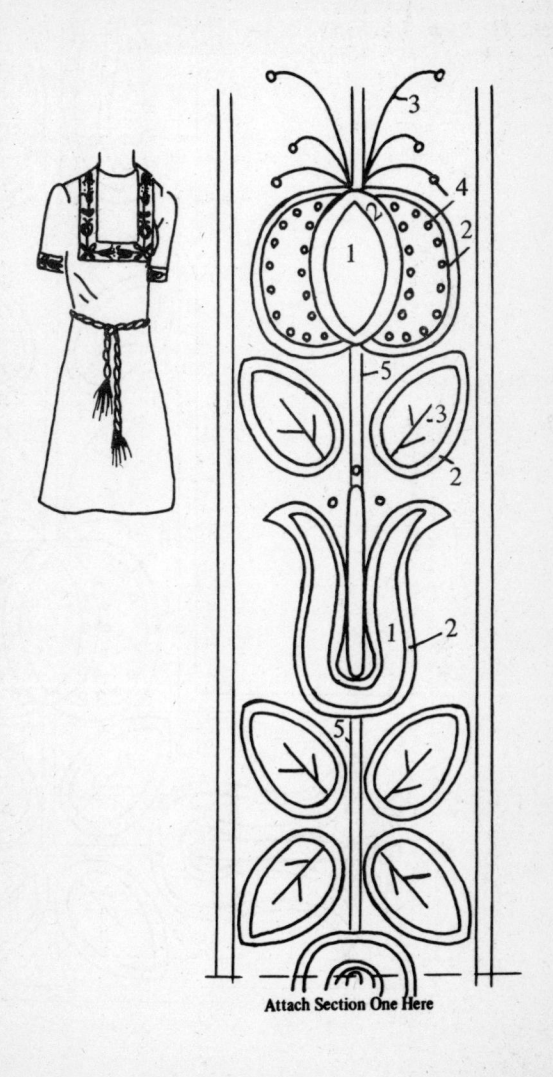

*Figure 77b.
Peasant Panel.*

Figure 77c. Stitch Key for Peasant Panel: (1) Satin stitch. (2) Buttonhole stitch. (3) Stem stitch. (4) French knot. (5) Chain stitch.

BOOTERY *(figures 78a – c):*

Be where fashion is—get yourself a pair of denim or canvas sham boots. (They slip into low cut shoes.) Or stop off at your favorite pattern counter and buy a spats pattern.

Materials: Purchased sham boots or spats pattern; stitchable fabric (not leather or plastic) to make spats; crewel or 3-ply yarns.

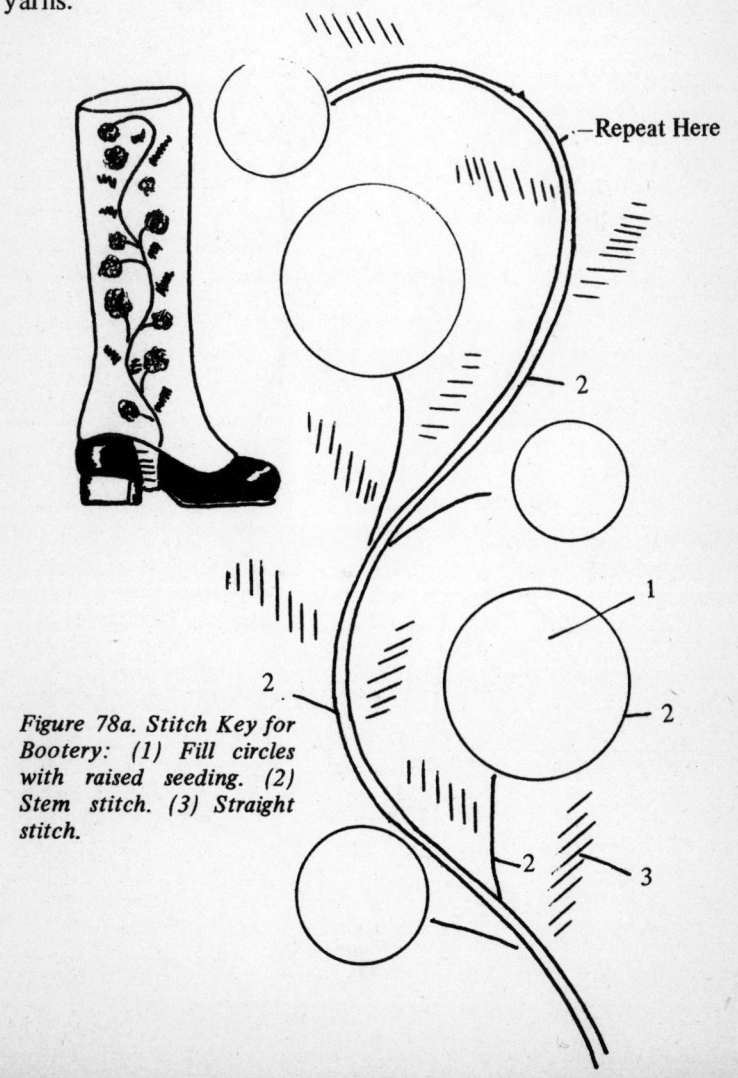

Figure 78a. Stitch Key for Bootery: (1) Fill circles with raised seeding. (2) Stem stitch. (3) Straight stitch.

138

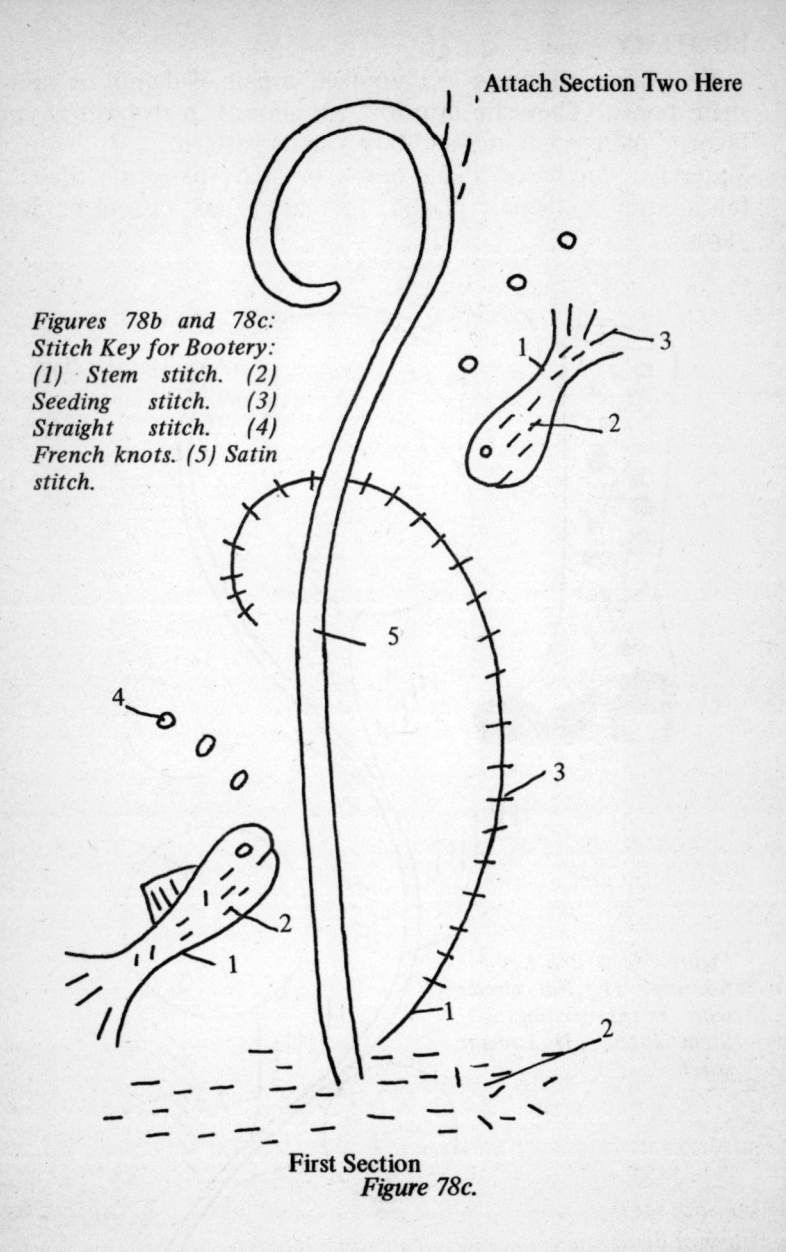

Attach Section Two Here

Figures 78b and 78c: Stitch Key for Bootery: (1) Stem stitch. (2) Seeding stitch. (3) Straight stitch. (4) French knots. (5) Satin stitch.

First Section
Figure 78c.

Second Section
Figure 78c.

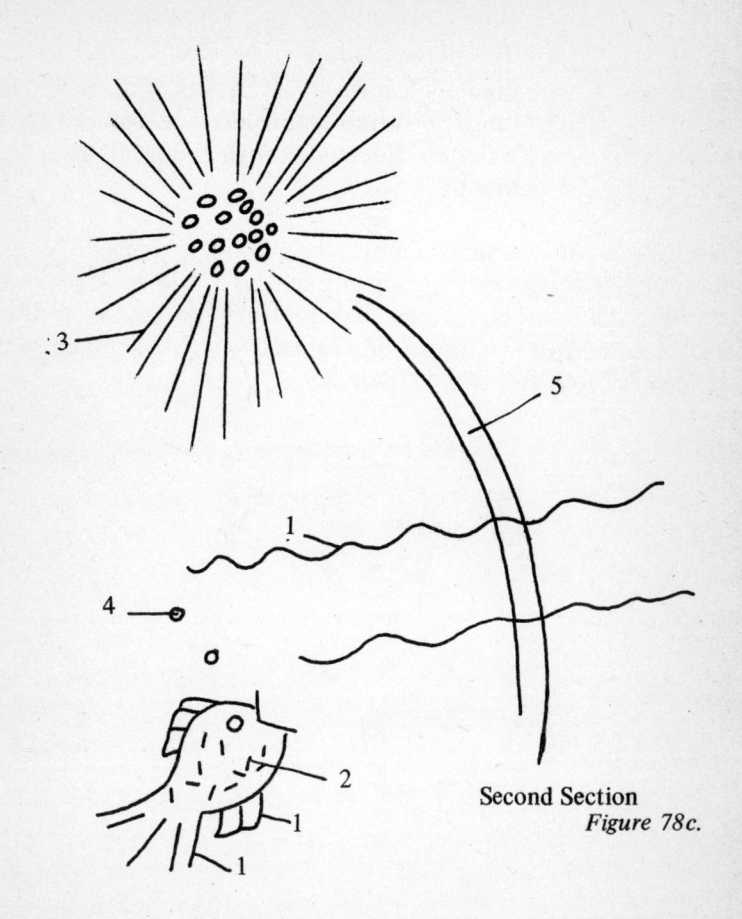

Directions: If making spats, construct following pattern directions. For both sham boots and finished spats, trace design and transfer using tissue paper and running stitch method. Be sure to put design on outside leg of each boot or spat.

The fish design is shown in two sections. Attach stem of second section where indicated on first section by dash lines. Flower design is repeated for desired length.

Embroider designs following stitch key.

BUTTON FACE *(figure 79)*:

It's a sleeve garter, an arm band or a topper for knee socks. It's a smiling face for a special place.

Materials: Cover your own button, 1½ inches in diameter; linen or similar weight fabric; 6-strand embroidery cotton or very fine yarns; ½-inch wide flat elastic long enough to just fit your upper arm or leg just below the knee.

Directions: Use a small embroidery hoop and piece of fabric just large enough to fit hoop. In center of fabric draw a circle 2-3/4 inches in diameter. Transfer face design to center of circle. Use 2 or 3 strands of embroidery cotton in needle to embroider face following stitch key.

Figure 79. Stitch Key for Button Face: (Mouth) Outline in stem stitch, fill in with

When embroidery is complete, cut out face on drawn circle. Sew a row of running stitches around edge of fabric. Center button on circle, with face accurately placed on button front. Pull thread tight; snap on back plate.

To make garter, cut a strip of fabric 2½ inches wide and 3 inches longer than elastic. Fold strip in half lengthwise. Turn in ¼ inch hems on all edges. Work a row of running stitches close to both long edges using embroidery cotton or yarn (Diagram I). Draw elastic throug the fabric strip. Overlap short ends and stitch securely together. Sew button face over seam to hide it.

MIRROR HANG-UP *(figure 80):*

Frame yourself in stitchery. Picture yourself in this mirror made with an embroidery hoop frame.

Materials: About ¼ yard of linen or linen-like fabric; 7-inch round embroidery hoop (wooden screw type); round mirror about 3 inches in diameter (mirror disks are often available in craft shops, through mail order craft houses or purchase an inexpensive mirror and remove it from the frame); crewel or 3-ply yarns; white liquid glue such as Sobo; cardboard; paste-on picture hanger.

Directions: Set fabric tightly in hoop. Be sure threads are pulled straight. Place mirror on center of fabric, draw around it lightly with pencil and set mirror aside. Trace leaf and flower design; transfer to fabric. Place them evenly spaced in a ring outside mirror circle. Follow sketch for placement of design or create something of your own. Remove fabric from hoop. Brush glue on outside of inner hoop section and inside outer hoop ring. Reset fabric in hoop with tension screw at center bottom of design. Be sure fabric is placed exactly in hoop as before. Let glue dry, then cut away excess fabric close to hoop.

Embroider design following stitch key. Then work a ring of Stem Stitch close to but just outside circle drawn for mirror.

Cut a cardboard disk the size of the inner hoop ring. Cut a fabric circle 1 inch larger than cardboard disk. Glue cardboard circle on center of fabric circle. Pull fabric taut with threads straight. Turn excess fabric over cardboard and glue to inside. Paste the fabric-covered circle to the back of the hoop frame.

142

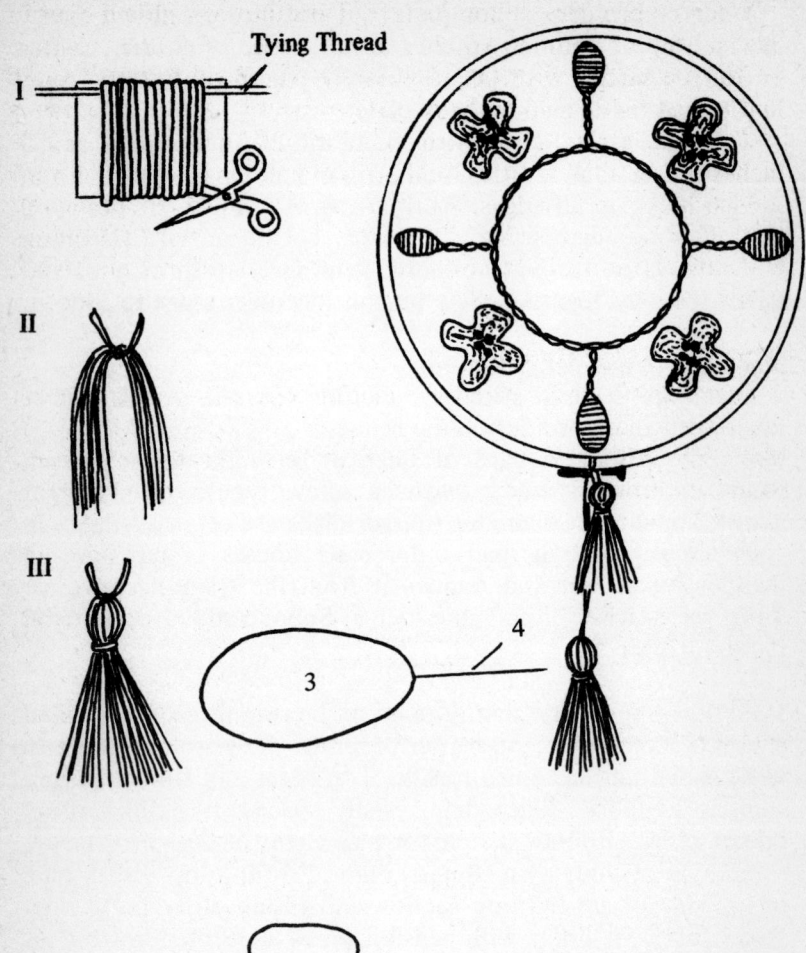

Tying Thread

I

II

III

3

4

1

2

Figure 80. Stitch Key for Mirror Hang Up: (1) Split stitch filling. (2) French knot. (3) Satin stitch. (4) Stem stitch.

When dry, glue on picture hanger. Turn over and glue mirror in place.

Make tassels, following Diagrams I–III. Wind yarn 40 to 50 times around a 4-inch piece of cardboard. Tie yarn strands tightly together at top with tying strand. Cut other end of strands. About ½ inch from top, tightly wrap a strand of yarn several times around tassels; tie and knot. Cut four strands of yarn each 12 inches long. Put them altogether and tie tassel to one end. Make another tassel and tie it to the other end. Attach tassel cord to mirror by winding it around the tension screw.

SQUARE THROW *(figures 81a – 1):*

Some call it an afghan, others a lap robe, still others a couch throw. Call it what you like, just make it square, and make it great. Finished throw will measure approximately 48 X 64 inches, including fringe (see page 155 for directions).

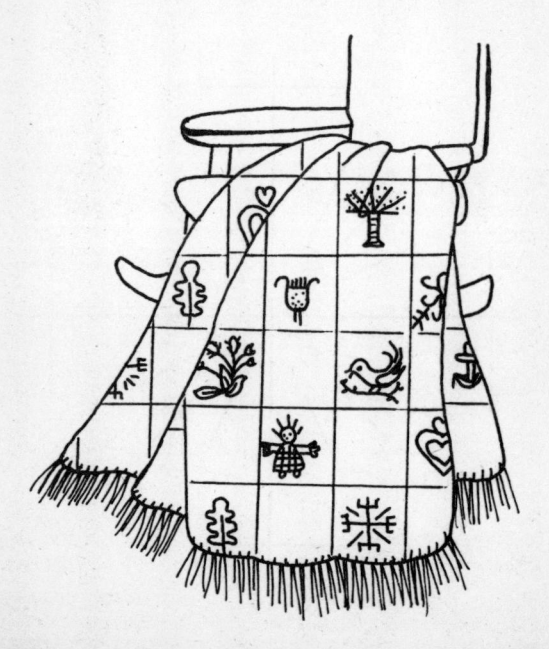

Figure 81a.

144

Figure 81c. Stitch Key for Square Throw—Design 2: (1) Straight stitch. (2) Satin stitch. (3) Stem stitch. (4) Lazy daisy. (5) Laid work, open tie with cross.

Figure 81b. (Opposite page.) Stitch Key for Square Throw—Design 1: All lines—chain stitch, dots—French knots.

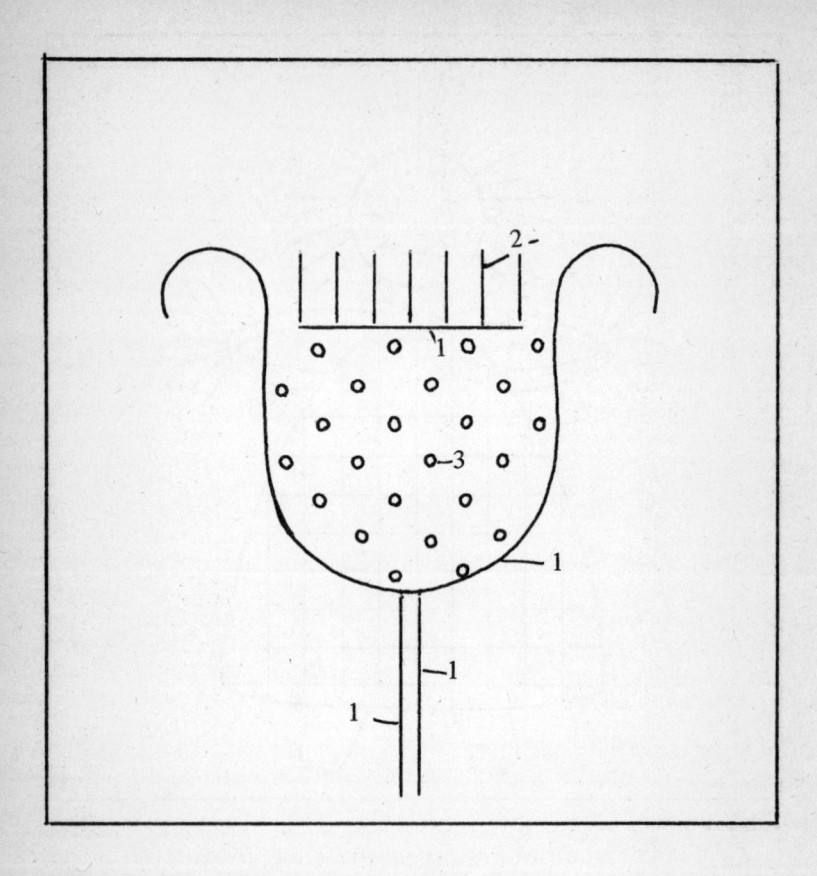

Figure 81d. Stitch Key for Square Throw—Design 3: (1) Chain stitch. (2) Straight stitch. (3) French knot.

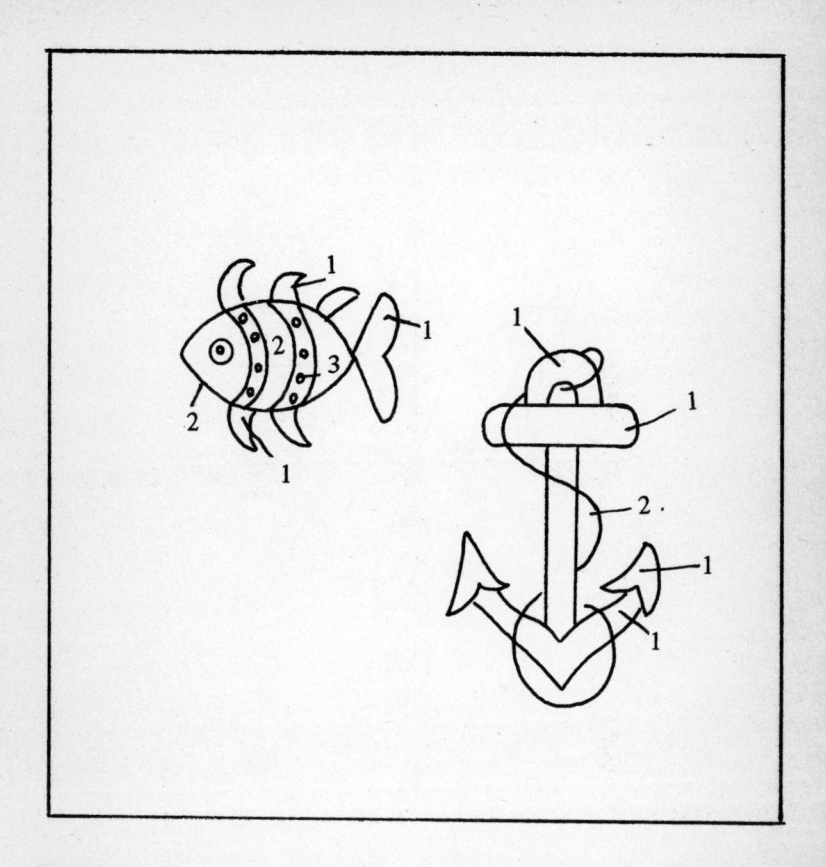

Figure 81e. Stitch Key for Square Throw—Design 4: (1) Satin stitch. (2) Stem stitch. (3) French knot.

Figure 81f. Stitch Key for Square Throw—Design 5: (1) Stem stitch. (2) Fern Stitch.

Figure 81g. Stitch Key for Square Throw—Design 6: (1) Stem stitch. (2) Lazy daisy. (3) Satin stitch. (4) French knot. (5) Seeding.

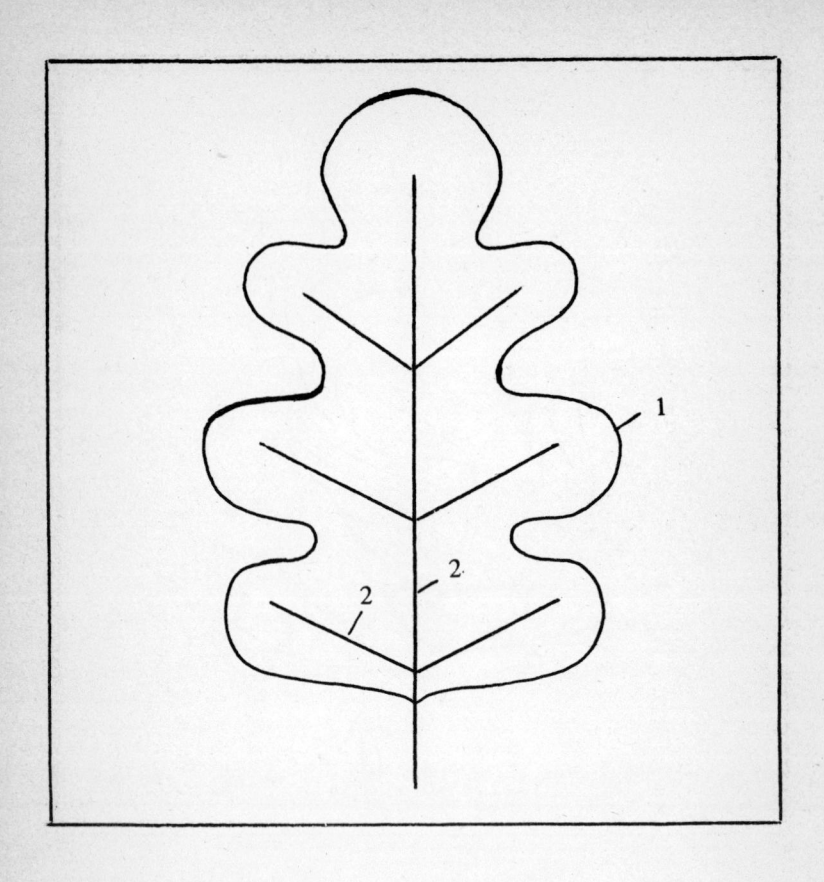

Figure 81h. Stitch Key for Square Throw—Design 7: (1) Chain stitch. (2) Stem stitch.

Figure 81i. Stitch Key for Square Throw—Design 8: (1) Laid work—open tied with diagonal stitch. (2) Satin stitch. (3) Stem stitch. (4) French knot.

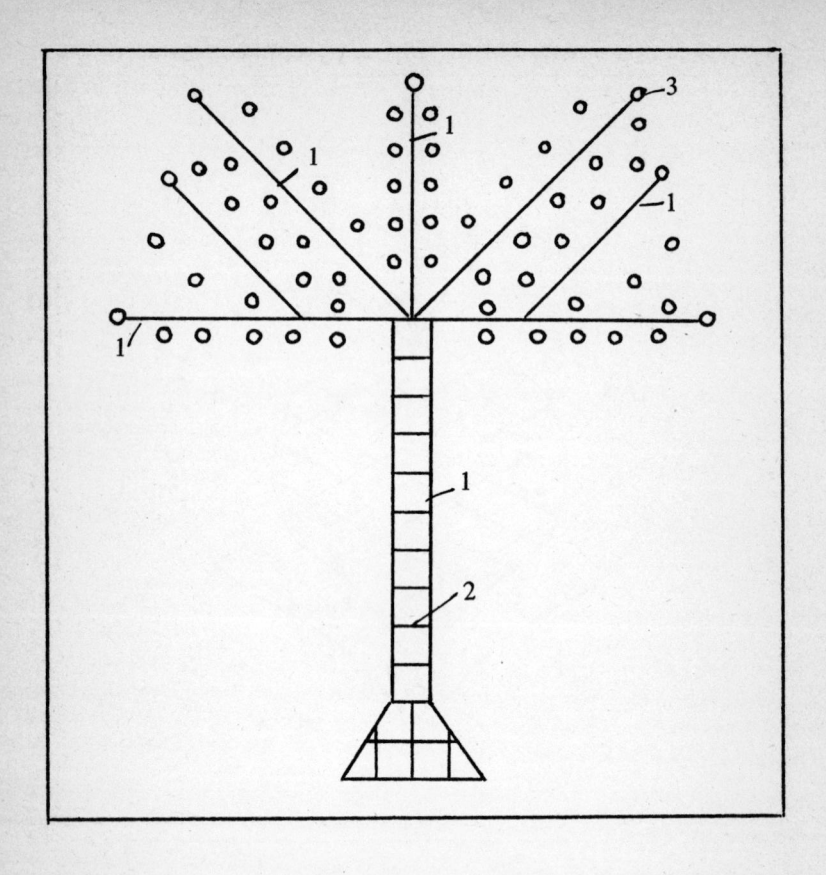

Figure 81j. Stitch Key for Square Throw—Design 9: (1) Chain stitch. (2) Straight stitch. (3) French knot.

Figure 81k. Stitch Key for Square Throw—Design 10: (1) Satin stitch. (2) Stem stitch. (3) Straight stitch. (4) Seeding.

Figure 81l. Stitch Key for Square Throw—Design 11: (1) Chain stitch. (2) Stem stitch. (3) Lazy daisy. (4) French knot.

SQUARE THROW *(Con't.)*

Materials: 1-3/4 yards of 45-inch wide, soft, light-weight woolen fabric (choose a firm weave); knitting worsted in black and assorted colors; yardstick; pencil; crochet hook.

Directions: Trim 1 inch off one raw edge of fabric so that fabric measures 62 X 45 inches. (This is necessary to make blocks come out even.) Be sure fabric is cut on straight threads. On raw edges, turn over ½ inch, then ½ inch again for hem; baste. Turn under ½ inch on selvage edges; baste. Your fabric should now measure 44 X 60 inches. Using black knitting worsted, Blanket Stitch complete edge of throw making stitches about ½ inch apart. Make fringe same as Paisley Shawl on page 90.

With yardstick and pencil (or basting thread), rule off 4 inch squares. First draw lines 4 inches apart across fabric, then draw lines 4 inches apart along the length of fabric. You should have 11 blocks crosswise and 15 blocks lengthwise.

Using black worsted, embroider all lines in Chain Stitch. First do all lines crosswise, then all lines lengthwise.

The eleven different designs are placed in the squares as shown in diagram I, starting with Design I in the top left hand square. These designs are the same or similar to traditional peasant symbols used for generations in embroidery, painting and other crafts. Use them for this throw, then use them on your wardrobe.

Trace designs and transfer them to their proper squares, using tissue paper and running stitch method of transfer. Be sure to center each design within its 4-inch square.

Embroider each design following stitch key.

HAVE A HEART *(figures 82a – i):*

Wear a heart on your sleeve. Put two on your vest. No matter how you break it, the heart is a sensational shape.

On this and following pages are a variety of heart designs to use where you choose. So stitch them here. Then stitch them there. Use knitting yarns, embroidery cotton and your special stitches.

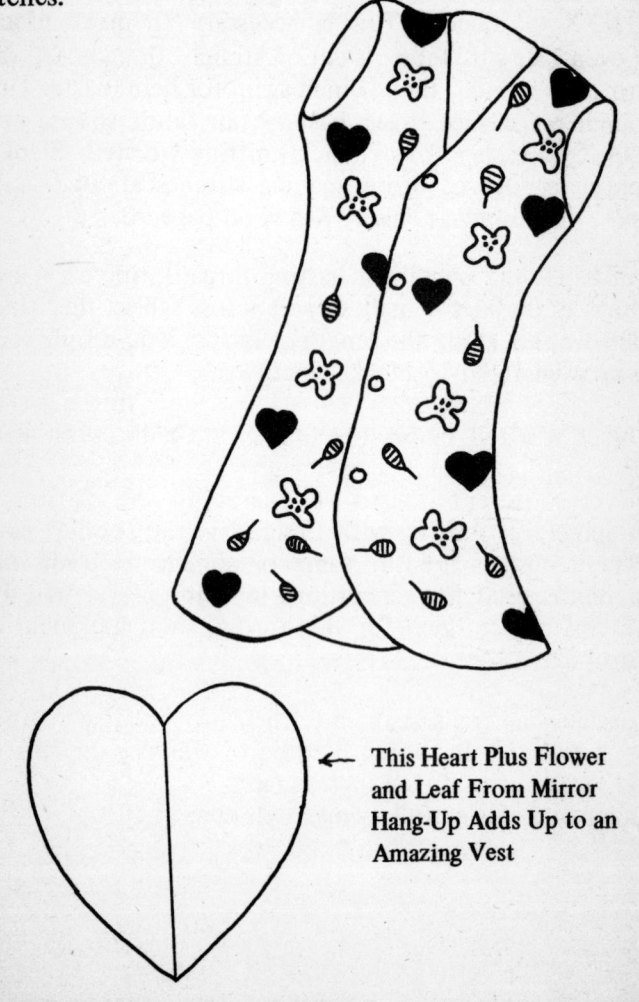

← This Heart Plus Flower and Leaf From Mirror Hang-Up Adds Up to an Amazing Vest

Figure 82a. Have a Heart—Design 1.

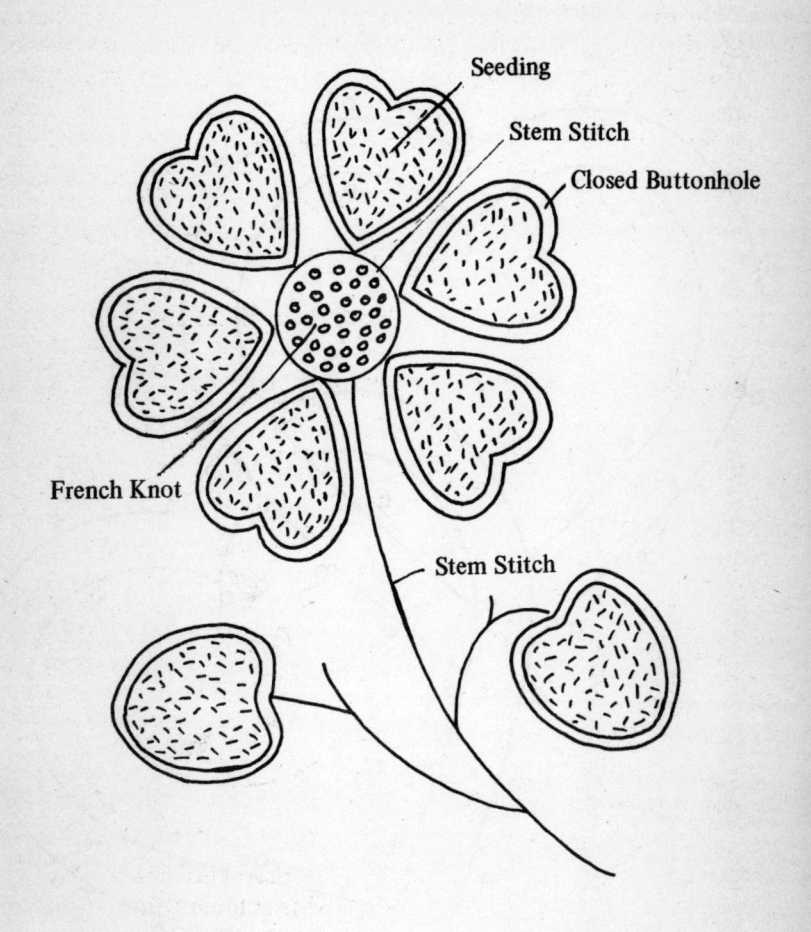

Figure 82b. Have a Heart—Design 2.

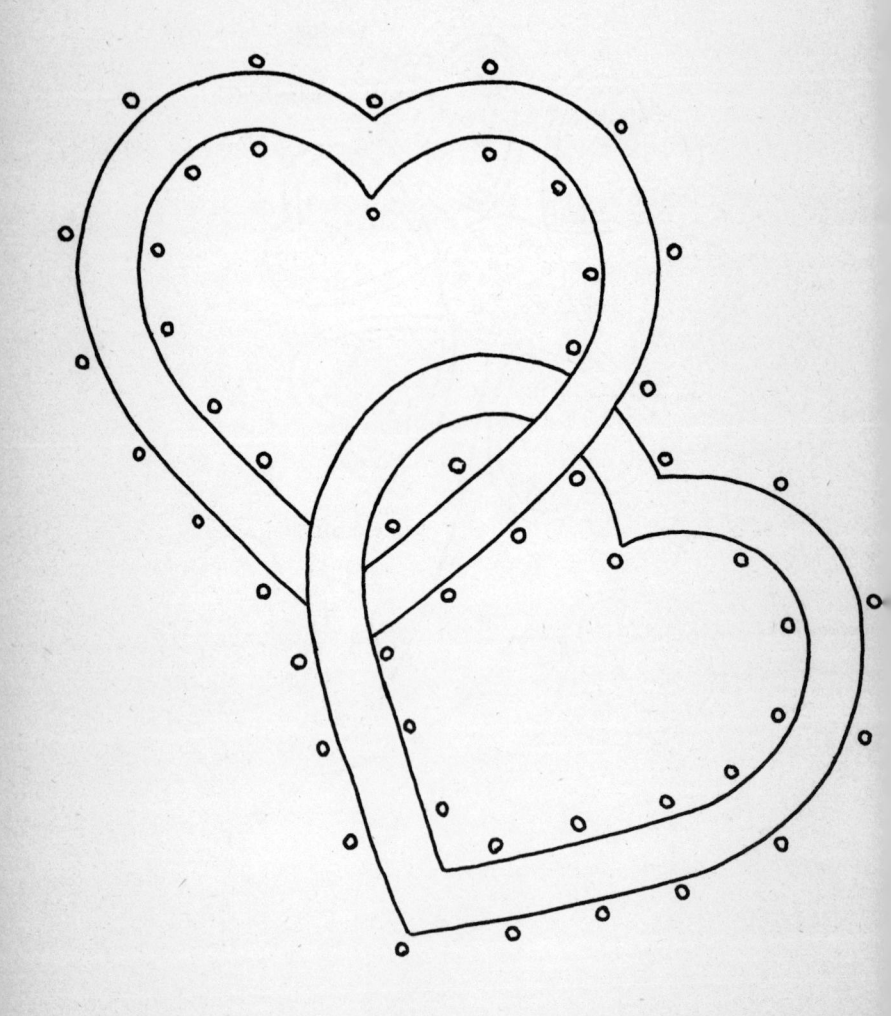

Figure 82c. Have a Heart—Design 3.

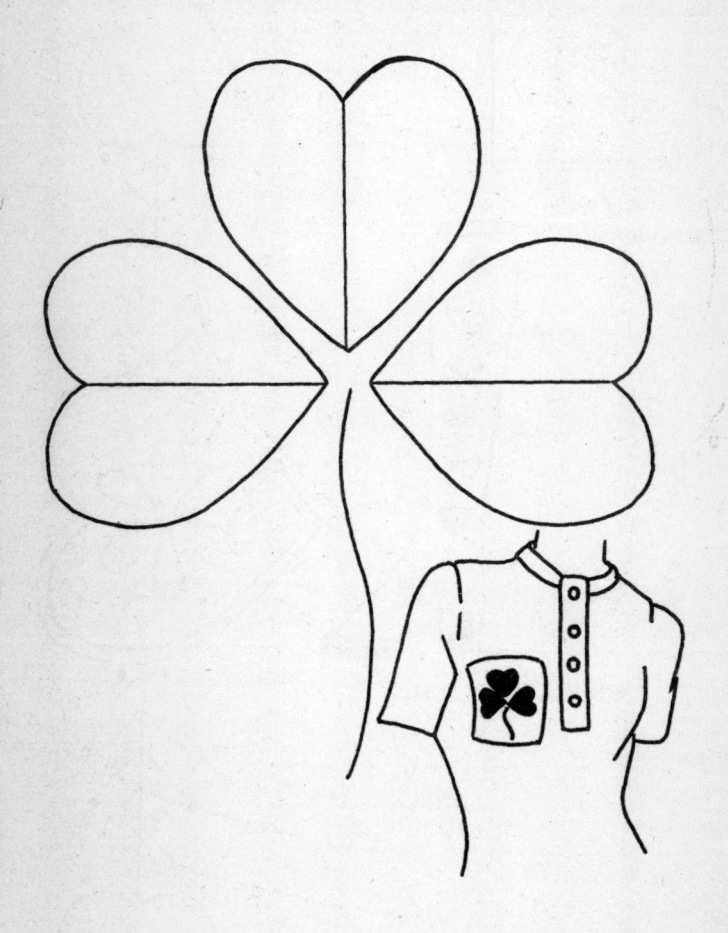

Figure 82d. Have a Heart—Design 4.

Got A Flap Patch Pocket on a Coat?

A Pair of Velvet Spats

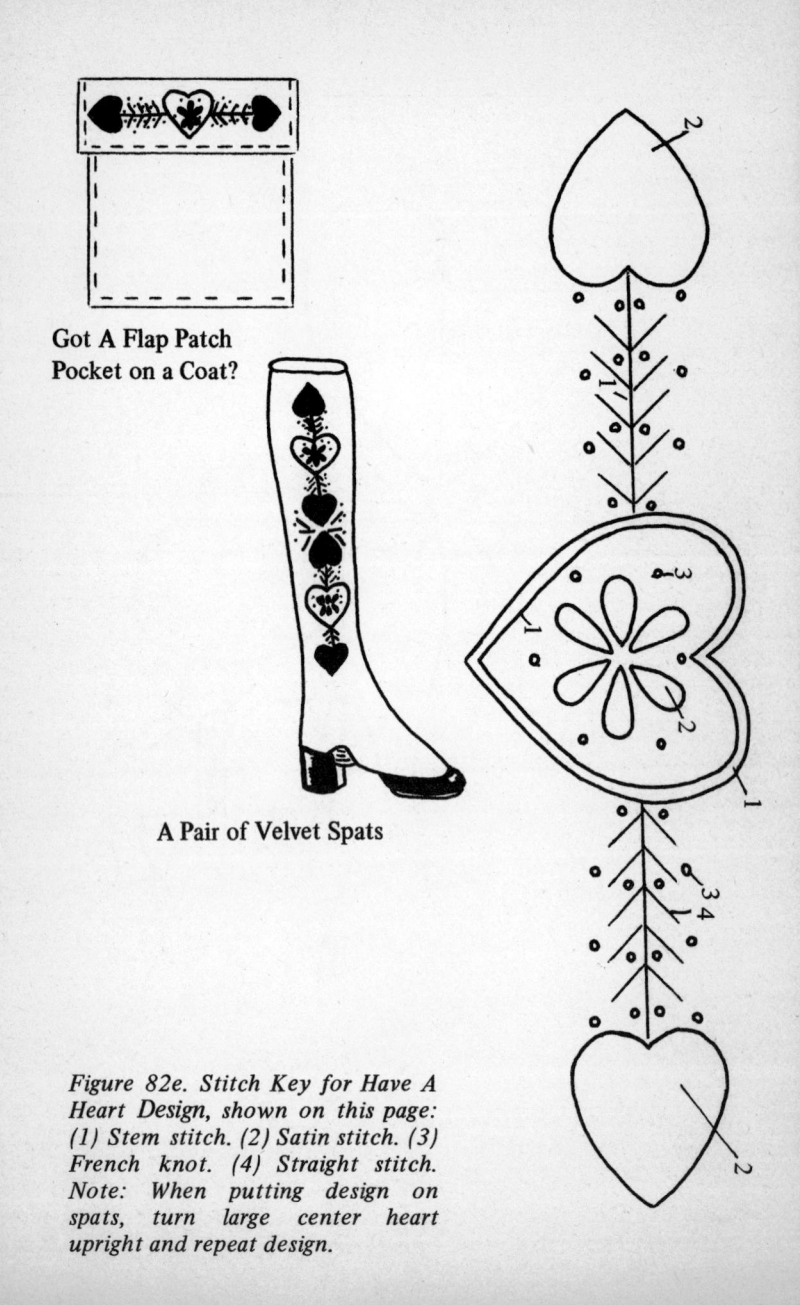

Figure 82e. Stitch Key for Have A Heart Design, shown on this page: (1) Stem stitch. (2) Satin stitch. (3) French knot. (4) Straight stitch. Note: When putting design on spats, turn large center heart upright and repeat design.

Figure 82f.
Have a Heart—Design 6.

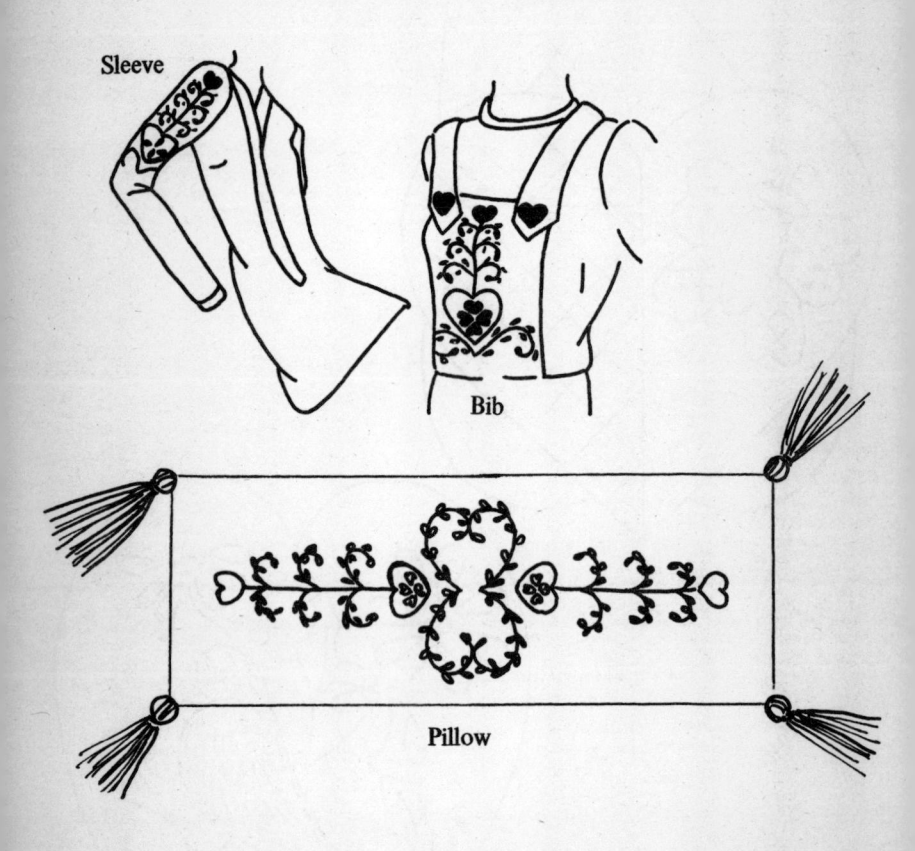

Figure 82g. Have a Heart—Design 7.

Figure 82h. Have a Heart—Design 8.

Figure 82i. Have a Heart—Design 9.

PRINT FABRIC PROJECT *(figure 83):*

Don't overlook printed fabrics when looking for material to embroider. With the design already there, the sky's the limit when it comes to ways of making designs stand up and be noticed. You decide what stitches to use or how much stitchery to apply. You could just outline several or all parts of a flower print with Stem Stitch or cover complete flowers with Satin Stitch. Or, if you have a large flower print, choose just a few random flowers to work on. A block print fabric allows you great freedom to put a variety of stitchery around the blocks or spot designs inside the blocks.

Let your imagination go wild.

Block Print Blouse
With Spot Designs

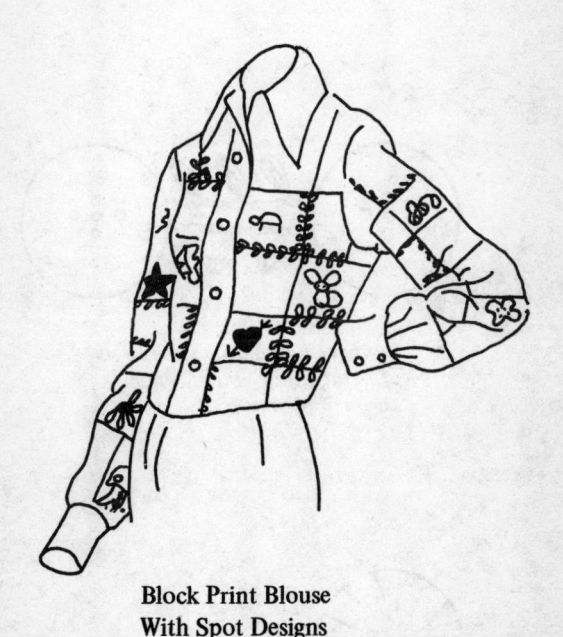

Figure 83. Print fabric project.

POLKA DOTS *(figures 84a and b):*

A polka dot print is a good spot to start a print fabric project. Just add a few lines, a few stitches, and spots turn on in many different designs. Try some of the ideas shown, then invent!

Work french knots around polka dots.

Connect polka dots with rows of petal stitch. Put French knots in center.

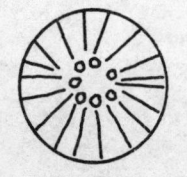

Straight stitches and French knots worked on dot.

Figure 84a.

167

Turn polka dots into daisys. Work lazy daisy stitch around dots.

Select random polka dots and make sun spots. Work nose in stem stitch. Dots in French knot. All other lines in straight stitch.

Figure 84b.

Figure 85.

DESIGNED FOR LARGE CHECKS *(figure 85):*

A bold black and white, large checked print fabric becomes unique when simple straight stitches are worked on alternate squares.

Purchase either yard goods or an already completed bedspread and drapes set. Transform the plain checks into little squares of interest. Use black pearl cotton for light weight fabrics or wool yarns for heavier weight. Work the design in black on the white squares, or in white on the black squares. Real ambitious? Work stitches on all the squares.

Figure 86.

SCARF TRICKS *(figure 86):*

Take a print scarf and dab it with stitches. Take a plain scarf and create an original. Scarves are in—wrap one around your head, your hat, your neck; tie one at your waist, your hips. Be a sizzler.

BELTED TUNIC *(figures 87a and b):*

Short, long, in-between. Make a tunic whatever length you wish. Choose a patterned fabric, then make the design live with a little or a lot of stitchery. Or, use a solid color fabric—like denim—and make your own creation with a stitchery design.

Materials: 1 yard print fabric for tunic (for 27 inch length, longer lengths will require more fabric); solid color fabric for lining; 2 large snap fasteners; 4 large buttons (optional); embroidery cotton or crewel yarns; large sheet of paper, pencil; ruler; sewing thread.

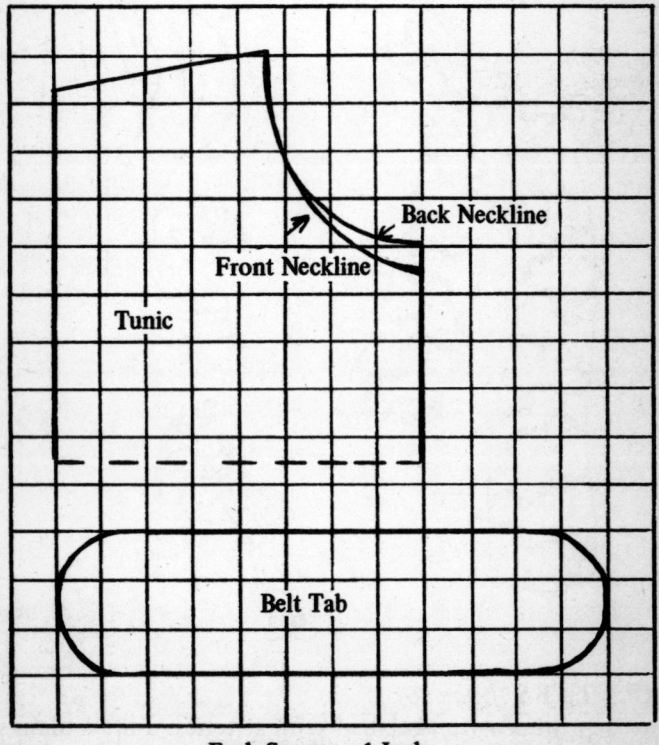

Each Square = 1 Inch

I

Figure 87a.

Figure 87b.

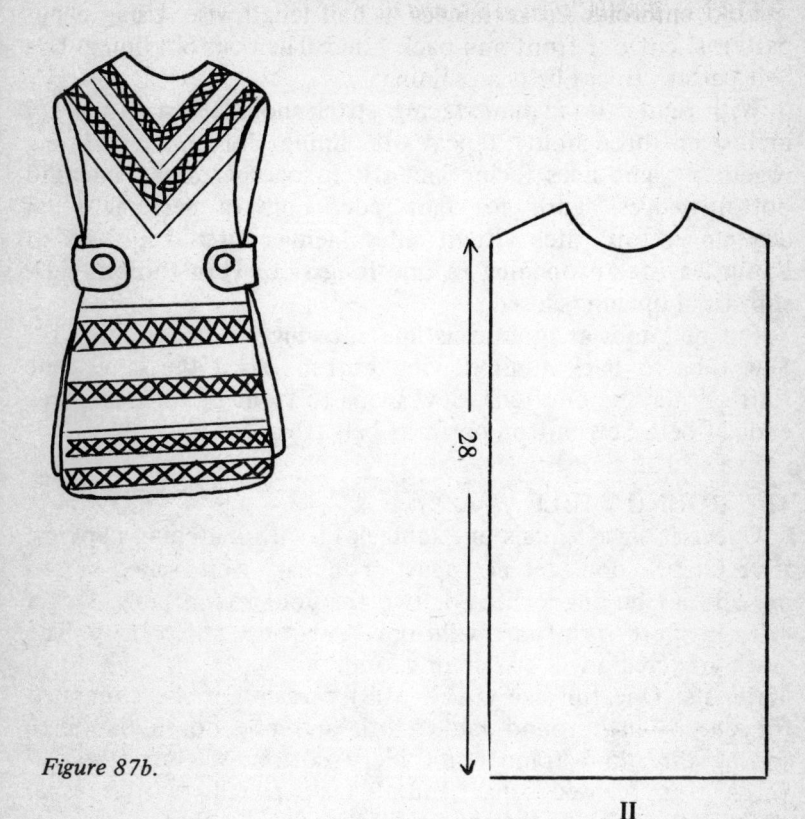

II

Directions: Tunic diagram is for small-medium size. For larger size, draw tunic pattern wider.

On paper ruled off in 1-inch squares, draw pattern of front and back neck and shoulder shaping and belt tab (diagram I). Make full size tunic paper patterns 28 inches long or desired length from shoulder to bottom edge (diagram II). Pin patterns together at shoulder; try on. Make any necessary adjustments before cutting fabric.

Cut two 18 X 29 inch pieces of fabric for tunic and two 14 X 5 inch pieces for belt tabs. Embroider print design as desired.

Fold embroidered rectangles in half lengthwise. Using paper patterns, cut out front and back tunic. Then cut out lining. Use belt pattern to cut belts and lining.

With right sides of tunic facing, stitch shoulder seam (make ½ inch seam throughout); repeat with lining. Put tunic and lining together, right sides facing and stitch together along side and bottom edges. Turn to right side. Fold in neckline seam allowance; top stitch. Right sides facing, stitch belt tabs to lining leaving an opening in one long side. Turn to right side, slip stitch opening closed.

Pin belt tabs at tunic waistline allowing for a loose easy fit. Sew tabs to back tunic sewing button on at the same time (button may be omitted). Sew snaps to front of tunic and free ends of belt. Sew button on front belt tabs.

THE ROUND TABLE *(figure 88)*:

One flat sheet equals one tablecloth with matching napkins. It's a fact. So don't let an August or January white sale pass you by without buying a sheet or two for your round table. Pick a print, a pretty print or a wild one. Cut it up; stitch it up. The cloth you create will be one of a kind.

Materials: One full-size (81 X 108) percale flat sheet (enough for one 40-inch round table cloth and one dozen napkins); sewing thread; 6-strand embroidery cotton; scissors; about 7 yards of purchased fringe; thumb tack; pencil; two pieces of string, one 40 inches long and the other 6-3/4 inches.

Directions: Open up all hems to add extra fabric inches. Wash sheet (most sheets shrink slightly); iron smooth.

Lay sheet out on the floor. Tie pencil to one end of the 40-inch piece of string; put thumb tack at the other end. Stick tack in center of upper left portion of sheet. Make a test swing, compass fashion, without making pencil lines to be certain tack is positioned correctly to draw the full 80 inch in diameter circle. When you're in the right spot, draw circle on sheet. Then draw 12 circles for napkins in the same way using the 6-3/4 inch string. Cut out cloth and napkins. Sew narrow hem edges by hand or machine. Sew fringe around table cloth edge.

13½" Diameter
Napkins

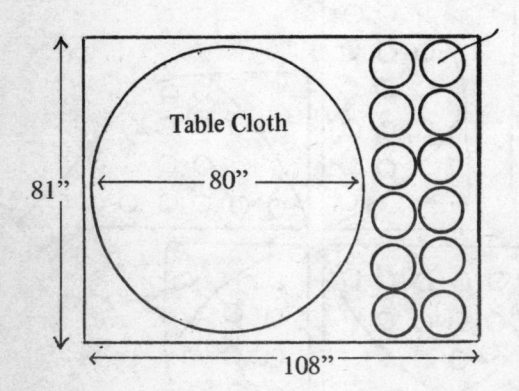

Figure 88. The Round Table.

Now do your own thing with stitches. Use all 6 strands of embroidery cotton in the needle.

Extra Note: Make a 72-inch round felt table cloth. Blanket Stitch the edge and add your own fringe. Couch a design in the cloth. Try the Artful Abstract design on page 85.

SPOT DESIGNS TO PUT ANYWHERE *(figures 89a – l):*

Pick a spot. Choose a design. Select a stitch. These designs are for putting anywhere. They're great for patches too.

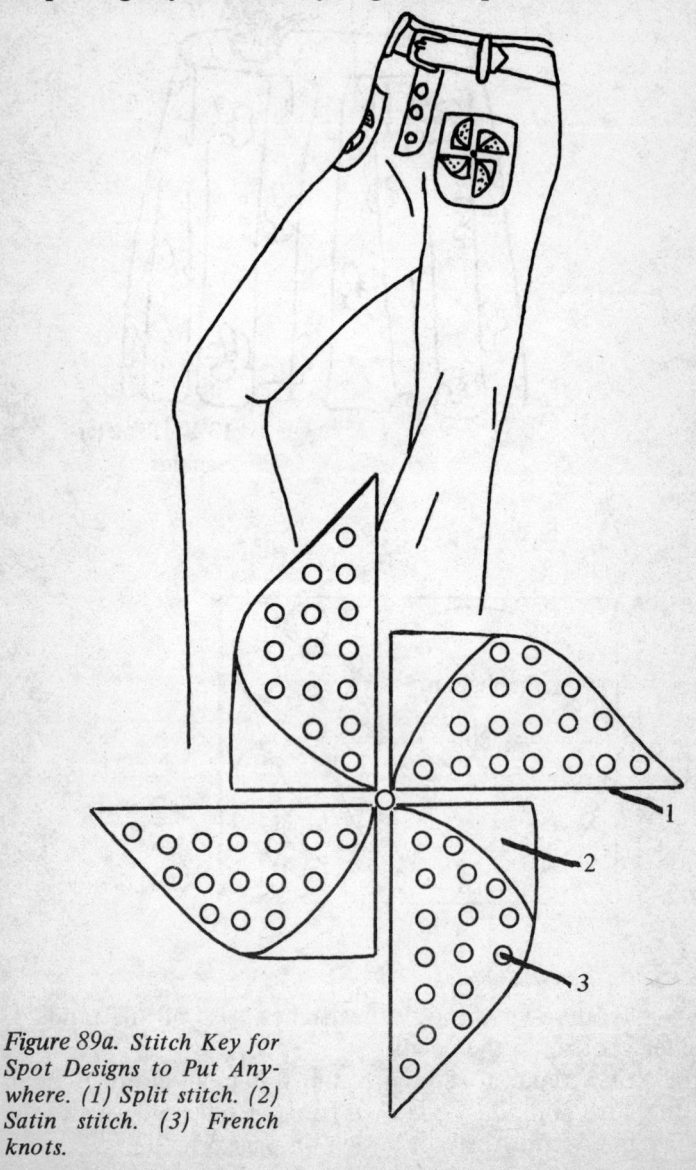

Figure 89a. Stitch Key for Spot Designs to Put Anywhere. (1) Split stitch. (2) Satin stitch. (3) French knots.

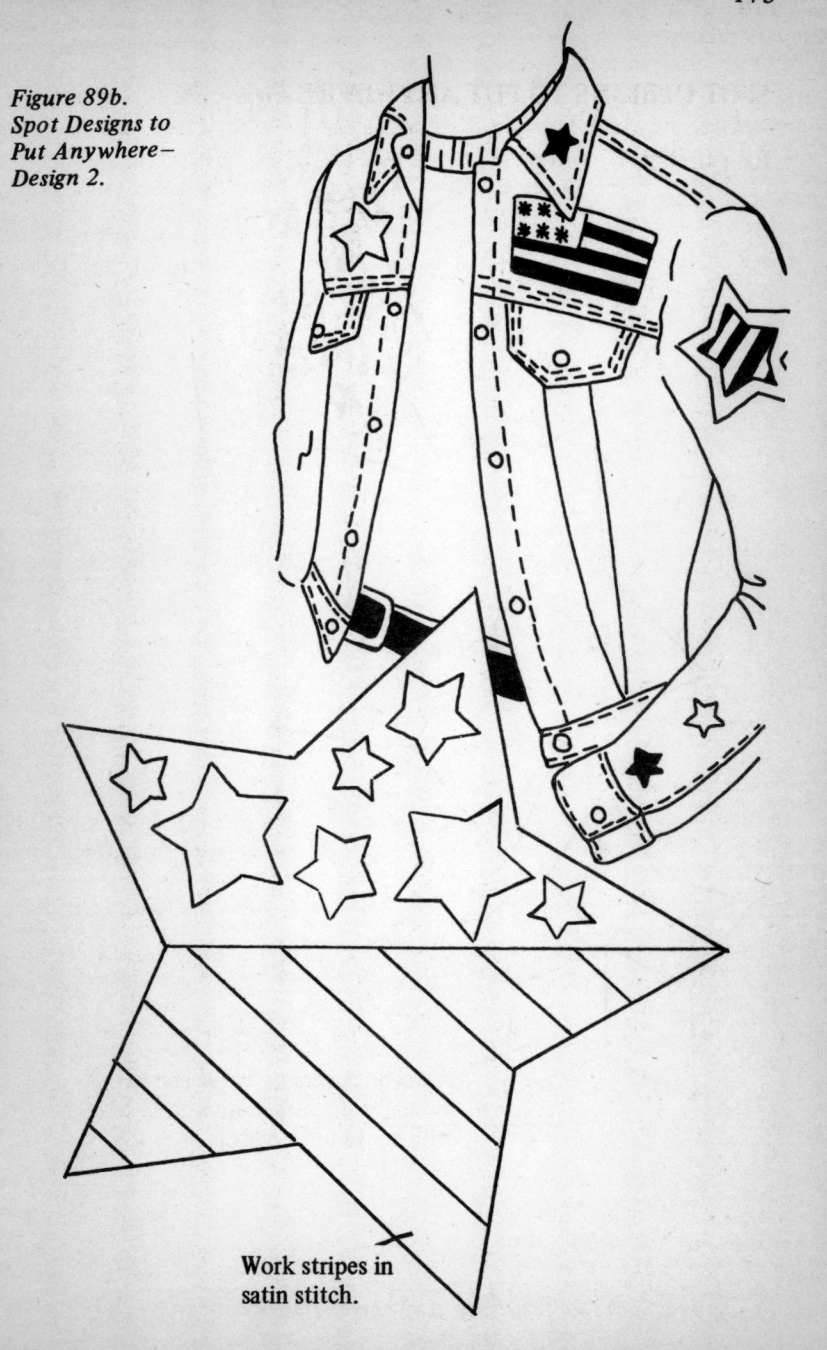

*Figure 89b.
Spot Designs to
Put Anywhere—
Design 2.*

Work stripes in satin stitch.

For solid coverage, divide star as shown, work each section in satin or fishbone herring.

Figure 89c. Spot Designs to Put Anywhere—Design 3.

Figure 89d. Spot Designs to Put Anywhere—Design 4.

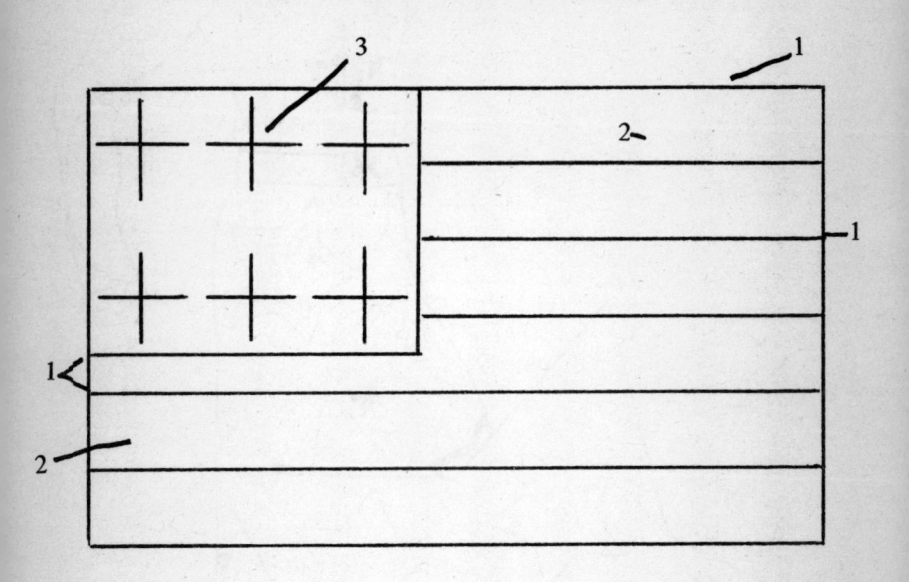

Figure 89e. Stitch Key for Spot Designs to Put Anywhere—Design 5, shown on this page: (1) Stem stitch—all straight lines in black. (2) Split stitch filling for stripes—red and white. (3) Star stich in bright yellow.

179

Figure 89f. Stitch Key for Spot Designs to Put Anywhere—Design 6: (1) Satin stitch. (2) Chain stitch. (3) Straight stitch.

Figure 89g. Stitch Key for Spot Designs to Put Anywhere—Design 7: (1) Satin stitch. (2) Buttonhole stitch. (3) Split stitch. (4) Seeding. (5) Straight stitch.

Figure 89h. Spot Designs to Put Anywhere—Design 8.

Figure 89i. Spot Designs to Put Anywhere—Design 9.

Figure 89j. Spot Designs to Put Anywhere—Design 10.

Figure 89k. Spot Designs to Put Anywhere—Design 11.

Figure 89l. Stitch Key for Spot Designs to Put Anywhere—Design 12, shown on this page: (Couch all lines except circle and beak). (1) Buttonhole stitch. (2) Satin stitch. (3) Split stitch filling. (4) Laid work—open. (5) Sheaf stitch filling. (6) Basket stitch filling (7) Stem filling. (8) Ermine filling. (9) Backstitch filling. (10) Cross stitch—double. (11) Split stitch. Enlarge on one inch squares.

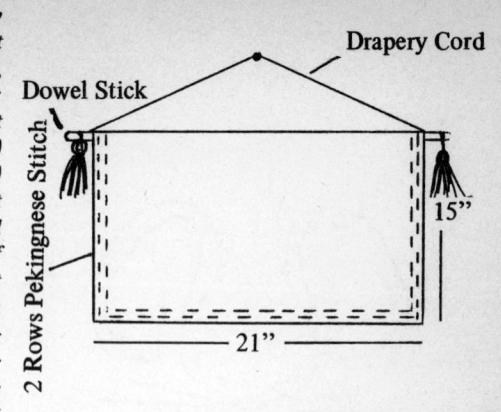

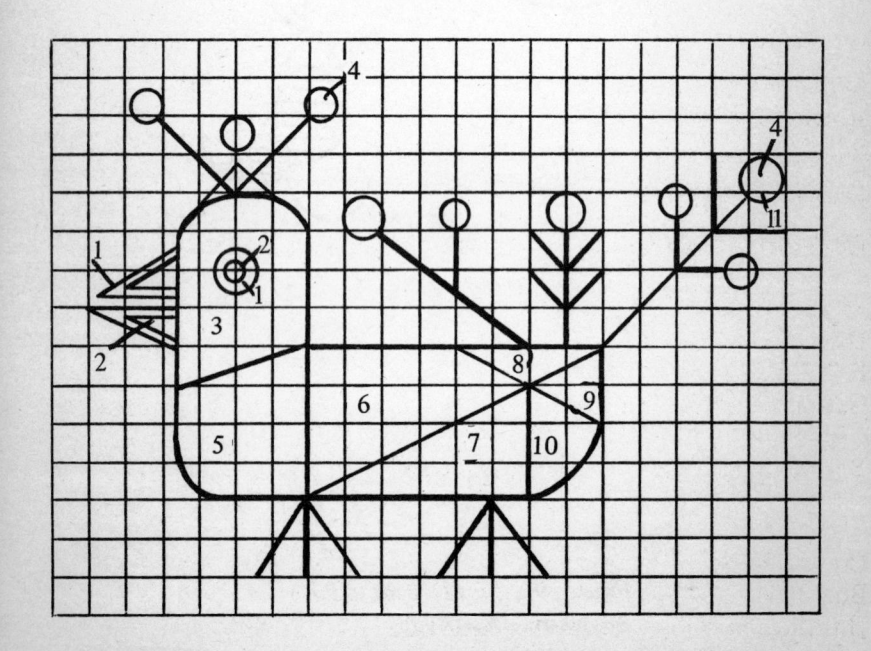

Chapter Five

Stitchery Suppliers

American Crewel Studio
Box 553
Westfield, New Jersey 07091

All supplies from fabrics to transfers. Catalogue available.

Dick Blick
P.O. Box 1267
Galesburg, Illinois 61401

Yarn craft supplier. Catalogue available.

Crewel World
Box 303
Huntingdon Valley, Pennsylvania 19006

Kits.

DMC Corporation
Elizabeth, New Jersey 07207

Will furnish name of supplier in your area for DMC threads and frames.

The Embroiderer's Guild
National Headquarters
30 East 60th Street
Room 1505
New York, New York 10022

Members can receive information about Guild branches, teachers, and supplies in the United States.

Herrschners, Inc.
Stevens Point, Wisconsin 54481

Yarns, transfer pencils, fabrics, hot-iron transfer patterns. Catalogue available.

House of Stitches
Box 547
Bainbridge, Georgia 31717

Kits.

In Stitches
P.O. Box 147
Miami, Florida 33165

Karla Stitcheries
P.O. Box 255
Sherwood, Oregon 97140

Kits. (Brochure 50c)

Kirsten's Danish Handicraft
P.O. Box 99012
Seattle, Washington 98199

Embroidery from Scandinavia.
Catalogue available.

Lejeune Incorporated
1060 W. Evelyn Avenue
Sunnyvale, California 94086

Free Catalogue.

Lily Mills Company
Shelby, North Carolina 28150

Yarns. Free catalogue.

Merribee
2904 W. Lancaster
Fort Worth, Texas 76107

General supplies. Free catalogue.

Needlecraft House
Wellesley, Massachusetts 02181

Kits.

Needlecraft House
West Townsend, Massachusetts 01474

Crewel yarns, linen, and general supplies. (Catalogue $1.00)

Needles 'N Hoops
Box 165
Abington, Pennsylvania 19001

Sampler kits.

The Niddy Noddy
1 Croton Point Avenue
Croton-on-Hudson, New York 10520

Olympus Thread Mfg. Co. Ltd.
8-9 Nishiki 3, Naka-ku
Nagoya, Japan

Excellent supplier of embroidery thread.

Paternayan Bros., Inc.
312 East 95th Street
New York, New York 10028

Distributor of imported wool threads and canvas. Will give name of nearest retail store.

Skon Embroideries
55 Lambert Lane
New Rochelle, New York

Kits. Catalogue available.

Jane Snead Samplers
Box 4909
Philadelphia, Pennsylvania 19119

Sampler kits.

Stitchendipity
Box 696
Commerce, Texas 75428

Kits and supplies.

Stitch Witchery
Route 10
Denville, New Jersey 07084

Classes and retailer for all supplies. No mail order.

The Stitchery
Wellesley, Massachusetts 02181

Crewel yarns, linen fabric and stitchery kits. Catalogue available.

Studio Twelve
1240 G Logan Avenue
Costa Mesa, California 92626

Kits.

Thumbelina Needlework Shop
1685 Copenhagan Drive
Solvang, California 93463

Kits.

Joan Toggitt Ltd.
1170 Broadway
New York, New York 10001

Threads and backgrounds. Can supply name of local retailer.

Transart
P.O. Box 126
Waynesfield, Ohio 45896

Design transfers available by mail.

Lee Wards
P.O. Box 206
Elgin, Illinois 60120

General supplies. Free Catalogue.

Wool-Art Studios, Inc.
Box 1005
Weston, Connecticut 06880

Kits.

THE FIRST IN LANCER'S NEW
CRAFT BOOK SERIES

THE COMPLETE BOOK OF DECOUPAGE

by
Frances S. Wing

#76305 $1.95

Discover the pleasures of decorating almost any object you wish with paper cut-outs easily obtained from magazines, newspapers, even wallpaper

THE COMPLETE BOOK OF DECOUPAGE

is filled with helpful hints, the latest innovations and techniques, and simple, step-by-step, fully illustrated instructions.

If this book is not on sale at your local newsstand send 10¢ for mailing costs to Lancer Books, Inc., 1560 Broadway, New York, N.Y. 10036. On orders of 4 or more books we pay the postage.
Write for free catalog, too!